Common
Law

To my parents, for all their encouragement

Common Good Law

Andrew C Ferguson
Solicitor and Notary Public

Avizandum Publishing Ltd
Edinburgh
2006

Published by
Avizandum Publishing Ltd
58 Candlemaker Row
Edinburgh EH1 2QE

First published 2006

ISBN 1-904968-09-0
      978-1-904968-09-2

British Library Cataloguing in Publication Data
A catalogue record for this book is available from the British Library.

Typeset by AFS Image Setters Ltd, Glasgow
Printed and bound by Bell & Bain Ltd, Glasgow

Contents

Appendices

Preface

I first heard of the common good as a legal concept in 1989, when I joined Kirkcaldy District Council as a solicitor. This was in itself surprising. I had already spent five years at university supposedly learning about the law of Scotland and a subsequent four years as trainee and junior solicitor with a private firm where a large part of my job was concerned with conveyancing.

Had all the transactions relating to common good somehow passed me by? Had I been asleep at the relevant bit of the degree course, and again during my diploma? Although this was possible, the odds of it seemed unlikely given that two sets of lectures covered property law and I had managed to stay awake often enough to pass the exams.

However, in the early months of my new job at the Council, common good seemed to be everywhere. As I blundered around the title safe in the Town House, Kirkcaldy (itself the subject of a key common good decision, as we will see) each former burgh in the District Council's area unveiled titles which were marked in the chartulary as belonging to "common good". An aura of mystery and romance hung over these title deeds in as much as an aura of mystery and romance can hang over any title deeds.

Finally, in around 1999, I set myself to understand the topic more fully. It struck me as a very interesting little nugget of property law which was, to me at least, both interesting and of practical relevance. I found it easier to write things down as I found them out and one version of this appeared as "Common Good Land" in 2000 SLT (News) 7.

However, as questions from both within my authority and other authorities continued to follow me, I realised that a lot more research and thought needed to go into the subject than the somewhat superficial approach I had taken in the article. In addition, there were some aspects of the article that I felt needed another look and, in particular, my emphasis of the *Murray v Forfar Magistrates* classifications over the *Ruthin Castle* doctrines on what constituted common good land.

In the brave new world of conveyancing reform in Scotland, with the feudal system having finally gone gently into the night and automated registration of title just around the corner, it might seem that a book on any aspect of the common good is somewhat anachronistic. I could well understand a point of view to the effect that the common good is little more than a historical appendix.

The analogy is an apt one. Like an appendix in the medical sense, common good is a topic that can lie dormant in the life of a local authority for quite some time and seem to serve very little purpose in the modern workings of the system. However, as several local authorities have found out to their cost, an appendix, when it decides to, can produce some painful consequences for the unwary, particularly, but not solely, in relation to disposal of land held on the common good.

With this in mind, I set myself the task of producing a book on the law of common good, which might allow common good property to retain its aura of romance without the accompanying mystery. In fact, much of the law surrounding common good is sound and sensible and, in true Scottish legal tradition, evolved over centuries of carefully reasoned and digested judgments in the Court of Session. Scots lawyers like to have their law founded on soundly reasoned principles and the good news is that, aside from the occasional statutory interventions, that is what common good law is founded on.

What I have attempted to do is give the law of common good an overall context both in terms of historical background and in relation to administration of the common good fund generally. I expect that most readers of this book will want to find out whether a particular piece of common good property can be disposed of and I have accordingly spent most time on common good land and its disposal. However, I hope that the remainder of the book, although of less practical relevance to the busy local authority conveyancer, will serve as a reasonable summary of the whole of this corner of the law.

The usual caveats for law books apply in full. As the Acknowledgements show, I am indebted to a great number of people for their help and support but I have no one to blame but myself for any mistakes. The law is stated as far as possible as at 4 November 2005.

Andrew Ferguson
February 2006

Acknowledgements

The usual saying that this book could not have been accomplished without the help and support of others is particularly true in this case.

First and foremost, I have to thank both SOLAR (Society of Local Authority Lawyers and Administrators in Scotland) and the Clark Foundation for their generous financial assistance. A book on such a specialised topic of Scots law was unlikely ever to sell in commercial quantities, and the grants received from these two organisations were a *sine qua non* of turning a pipe dream into a printed volume.

SOLAR's membership also gave assistance in non-financial, but equally important, ways. I would like to thank them all for their unfailing enthusiasm and encouragement, as well as practical assistance in digging out information on cases past and present. All those who took the time and trouble to complete the survey helped contribute to what I hope is at least an interesting set of results at Appendix V. It is invidious to single anyone out amongst the many who helped me, but Hazel Lawson, Graeme Korn, Margaret Allan and Burns Shearar deserve a special mention.

Thanks are due to counsel who allowed me to refer to opinions which they had given to other local authorities, as also the authorities themselves. For obvious reasons the cloak of anonymity covers them but they know who they are. Similarly, Professor Rennie was kind enough to allow me to refer to his opinion in the *South Lanarkshire* case.

In my own authority, I would like to thank my legal bosses past and present for their encouragement and understanding. I hope that at least some of the knowledge I have gained in the research for this book can be on call for them for a little longer.

A number of non-legal luminaries have given various kinds of help to me in the writing of this book. Michelle McDermott's patience in typing the first draft of the manuscript and helping with the redrafting was immense: I really could not have completed the job in any sort of timescale without her. Eileen Rowand, Team Leader in Fife's Finance and Asset Management Service, was good enough to read through and comment on an early draft of chapter 3.

Margaret Cherry in particular at Avizandum has shown great faith in a project which, as indicated, is unlikely to be a big moneyspinner for the publisher. Her helpful advice and comments have been a constant throughout the process.

It is traditional to acknowledge the long-sufferingness of book widows and orphans but Alison and Heather have been particularly long suffering in putting up with my absences.

Last but by no means least, Professor Roddy Paisley was a tremendous encouragement to me in the early stages of putting this book together; as with all those who helped me, I hope I've lived up to his expectations with the final product.

Tables of legislation

Table of statutes

Table of orders, rules and regulations

Table of cases

Chapter 1

Origins and definitions

1.1 Historical origins of common good

The common good is a fund of money and assets administered by local authorities in respect of each former burgh within the area of that authority. Although it is administered separately from other local authority funds for accounting purposes, it is owned outright by the local authority[1]. The immediate reason for this separate treatment is the provisions of the Local Government (Scotland) Act 1973[2]. However, the roots of common good – and the issues it raises today – stretch back much further.

In its most basic form, common good has its origins in the early Middle Ages, when the *ferm toun* – a small settlement of inter-connected families living in close proximity for mutual protection and support – took a collectivist approach to certain aspects of the farming operation.

The principal feature of this approach was the *common muir*. Although individuals might have their own strips of land radiating out from the settlement for arable use, it made sense to share graz-ing land for herd animals. With the advent of the feudal system, this land was often feued out in common for specific purposes. Other essential pertinents, such as peat-cutting rights, or land set aside in the centre of the *toun* for bleaching and drying clothes, were also owned in common.

Distinctions between *commonties* such as these and common good

---

1 Local Government (Scotland) Act 1973, s 222. See the further discussion of this point at **1.4**.
2 See chapter 2.

in its later form are discussed below[3]. However, the common good
itself and its development as a legal concept matches its historical
development, and in particular the evolution of such simple *ferm
touns* into burghs.

Scottish burghs (derived from the Anglo-Saxon *burh*) derived
from a desire on the part of mediaeval Scotland to develop eco-
nomically. In the early 1100s, the Scottish kings imported ideas,
people and material wholesale from Continental Europe in an
effort to modernise and improve the Scottish economy.

David I, in particular, introduced a number of measures which
built on the newly arrived feudal system and reflected what he had
seen during his time on the Continent. His wholesale encouragement of monastic orders such as the Cistercians and the Knights
Hospitaller and Templar, for example, was not entirely for reasons
of piety. The monasteries brought with them the latest ideas in a
number of industries such as farming and wool trading. They also
connected Scotland to their own international trading networks.

David I is also thought to have settled Flemish traders in large
numbers in places such as Ayrshire, Fife and Lothian because of
their connections with important markets in the Low Countries
and their expertise in the import/export trade. The concept of a
burgh was stimulated by such settlers and became an ideal model
for creating and controlling economic activity – both for the
Crown and the inhabitants.

The burgh was in some senses the mediaeval forerunner of a
trading company. Likeminded trades people pooled their resources
to create an infrastructure which assisted their business. At the same
time, linked operations such as fishermen and boat builders, for
example, or blacksmiths and woodworkers, were able to create
networks of mutual benefit.

A grant by the Crown or the local feudal baron of burgh status
provided a geographical and economic focus for such activity.
Important rights such as harbourage, the ability to hold markets
and impose tolls gave the burgh revenue-raising ability. The grants
of land which went with a burgh charter gave the bailies, or magis-

---

3 See **1.2**.

trates, an opportunity to control development and reserve infra-structural requirements such as roads and market squares.

Initially, all revenues raised by the burghs went to the Crown. However, gradually burghs came to be granted *feu ferme* status, paying a fixed *reddendo* to the granter of the charter. This allowed the bailies of the burgh to raise revenue above and beyond the fixed figure, and raise capital by disposing of plots of land to revenue-producing burgesses. These sums were paid into a common fund to be used for the purposes of the burgh. As burghs proliferated throughout the land, such funds became known by the purpose they were intended for: the common good.

Burghal administration, as a form of local government, was to remain for centuries. Common good property – whether mon-etary or land-based – was at the epicentre of a burgh's prosperity. By definition, it had to be used for the benefit of a burgh's inhabi-tants, or the entire burgh stood to fail. However, that was not always necessarily the case in practice.

The coming of the Agricultural and Industrial Revolutions changed economic realities in burghs as elsewhere. Although the Convention of Scottish Burghs retained some political clout due to the outdated electoral system, capital became concentrated in the hands of individual entrepreneurs rather than trade guilds or burgh councils themselves. Economic activity moved to areas that suited particular industries – proximity to a river or a canal, for example – rather than necessarily within the burgh boundaries. Burghs were frequently run by the placemen of commercial interests.

At the same time, the influx of larger populations into towns increased the need for local government to deal with infrastructural requirements, housing, town planning and so on. There was also a need for increased professionalism in the performance of civic functions: Edinburgh's first firemaster, for example, was appointed shortly after the Great Fire of 1824 demonstrated how ineffective and disorganised the existing arrangements for firefighting were. Professional police forces came into existence around the same time.

There was also increasing unrest at the way the common good was being used by those in charge. A Commission published in

1836[4] uncovered widespread corruption and use of common good assets for personal gain by the magistrates. The Whig reformers of the early 1830s saw that the mediaeval burgh was no longer fit for purpose as a unit of local government and began a long series of legislative reforms with the Representation of the People (Scotland) Act 1832 and the Royal Burghs (Scotland) Act 1833. It was the start of a series of reforms which was to culminate, 140 years later, with the abolition of burghs altogether in the Local Government (Scotland) Act 1973.

At the same time, public health, housing and other essential functions were entrusted to the burgh magistrates. The common good became only part of the answer to the burgh's problems.

A corollary of this change was a change in attitudes of the inhabitants towards the burgh's patrimony. The authorities, from being the board of directors of a common trading operation, had become a more distant corporate body surrounded by legislative powers and paid officials. The stage was set for a conflict with deep ideological roots, played out through numerous legal challenges to the authority of the magistrates and others.

An example of this process can be found in the facts of *Grahame v Magistrates of Kirkcaldy*[5]. Over the preceding centuries, the magistrates had used the land granted in the burgh charter to sell off small plots to the residents, creating the herringbone street pattern common to many mediaeval Scottish burghs. In 1754, the remaining land was conveyed to the Lord Provost under the condition that a third of the area was to be reserved for recreation and the drying of linen cloth. This condition remained in the title when the Provost reconveyed the land to the burgh in 1788.

By the 1870s the land, from being an area used for various things including the drilling of volunteers, had declined into a derelict piece of waste ground, part of which was used as a dunghill. This was partly due to the neglect of the local authority, a point returned to when the case is discussed in **8.1**. Another reason was that mid-Victorian development had taken away the focus of activity from the original street pattern uphill and northward.

---

4 Royal Commission on Municipal Corporations in Scotland (1836).
5 (1879) 6 R 1066.

However, when the magistrates proposed building police stables on the land, a resident of the burgh objected, and took the case to the Court of Session. In a landmark decision discussed in more detail later[6], the court upheld Mr Grahame's petition. What is important to note here is how a once key part of the burgh's mediaeval landholding had become so irrelevant that it was being used as a dunghill. However, it still remained important enough in other senses for one of the residents to object to its being used by the burgh for more modern purposes.

Paradoxically, as the shrinking areas of land forming part of burgh charters became subject to new pressures, new sources of common good land were appearing. In an effort to repay their home town for hosting their industries, many local industrialists and other landowners granted land to the burgh for behoof of the common good of the inhabitants of the burgh. Parks, museums, libraries and other recreational facilities were often endowed in this way in the late nineteenth and early twentieth centuries. Often, the wording in the title makes it clear what the magistrates could, and could not, use the land for.

The economic history of a burgh, accordingly, provides an appropriate overall context for the common good and its origins. Buildings formerly dedicated to civic uses, land used from time immemorial for public purposes, and the later addition of gifts and endowments by factory owners and other philanthropists form the three main types of property held by local authorities today as part of their common good.

More than that, the historical origins of the land and buildings on a burgh's common good account give a clue as to why local authorities' treatment of them can still rouse such strong local emotions.

Disposal of such property can recall a long time ago when government was more locally based and a burgh was, to an extent at least, master of its own destiny. Alternatively, proposed disposal of land endowed by a Victorian factory owner can bring to mind the original philanthropic ideals behind the gift, as well perhaps as

6 See **6.4** and **8.1**.

the hard labour extracted from the populace in return for it. And the widespread corruption and cronyism of burgh administration historically has created a climate of suspicion of the authorities' motives well in advance of today's cynicism about politics.

This chapter having looked at the origins of the burghs which produced the common good, chapter 2 will look at the various attempts to control use of the common good from the late nineteenth century onwards. In the meantime, however, it is necessary to delineate exactly what some of the terms used above mean in the legal context.

1.2   Types of burghs and commonties

The historical introduction above gives only a very brief overview of how burghs came into existence and their role in the delivery of local government over several centuries. For a more detailed introduction, see paragraphs 9 to 22 of the Local Government title in volume 14 of the *Stair Memorial Encyclopaedia*. For those more interested in the historical viewpoint, some further reading is suggested below[7]. Readers may also find in many cases that, to fully understand the process by which a town became a burgh and what might be comprised within its common good, the best source material can be found in local history books.

However, for the hard-pressed lawyer trying to find an answer to a modern-day problem, all this history has left a legacy of specialist terms which only help to add to the mystique of the common good. Some of the more frequent ones are defined briefly in the following paragraphs.

Royal burghs

Royal burghs are burghs created by a charter to the bailies or magistrates direct from the Crown. Although the term "royal"

---

7 For a general introduction, see Michael Lynch, *Scotland: A New History* (1992). For the later development of the burgh, see T M Devine, *The Scottish Nation 1700 to 2000* (1999).

burgh does not appear until 1401, there were undoubtedly burghs created by Crown Charter before then and their rights were preserved in the Treaty of Union 1707 between England and Scotland[8]. Royal burghs had more extensive powers than burghs of barony or regality but each varied according to the terms of the charter. Paradoxically, in the later life of burghs, inconsistencies in taxation gave royal burghs a competitive disadvantage compared with the "lesser" burghs. There were, at least at one point, seventy-two royal burghs.

Burghs of regality

As discussed at **1.1**, the king was not the only person to recognise the economic advantages of having traders organised into burghs. From the fourteenth century onwards, the Scottish Crown gave grants of land *in liberam regalitatem* to trusted adherents. Grants of large tracts of land in this way in general came with greater rights as the recipients were seen as key strategic partners who could be trusted to dispense everything including justice, up to, but not including, the right to try for treason. Burghs created by these magnates are known as burghs of regality.

Burghs of barony

One step down from the lords of regality, the barons also were able to create burgh status even if the powers conferred were lesser than royal burghs. Such burghs often still had the right to hold burghal courts and create monopolies of trades and crafts. Both of these activities were, of course, sources of income for the common good.

Parliamentary burghs

The Representation of the People (Scotland) Act 1832 amended burghal representation to Parliament as part of the first set of

8 Articles XVII–XXI.

moves intended to offset the "rotten burgh" electoral system. Of fifty-three Members of Parliament, twenty-three were representatives of burghs under the reforms. The term is unlikely to be used in title deeds now but may crop up from time to time in local histories.

Police burghs

For a large part of the nineteenth century, certain functions such as police were administered separately from burghal administration by means of statutory commissioners. Police burghs were those created under the Burgh Police legislation prior to the Burgh Police (Scotland) Act 1892[9], which amalgamated overall burgh administration into one unit. Confusingly, the reference to "police burghs" in the 1892 Act, Part II, is not to the burghs created by the prior legislation at all but to the new units created in former royal burghs or burghs of barony or regality by amalgamating the burghs with the police commissioners for the same area[10].

Commonty

Commonty is the term most likely to give rise to confusion in relation to land held on the common good. Strictly speaking, a commonty consists of an area of ground used by a discrete number of landholders in common, often as part of their grant from the local landowner. Many commonties reach back to the original infield/ outfield system of farming where the herds were grazed on the common muir. Commonties could exist within and outwith the burgh itself, and might be shared between settlements.

In this way, then, areas of commonty are frequently both the

---

9 For example, the General Police and Improvement (Scotland) Act 1862, s 3, which enabled "populous places" under 700 to form themselves into burghs.

10 See Muirhead, *Municipal and Police Government in Scotland* (3rd edn) for a commentary on the Act. Part II of the Act gave rise to considerable confusion and was reworked by the Town Councils (Scotland) Act 1900, s 5.

forerunner and contemporary of what is now known as common good land. As far back as 1695, the Division of Commonties Act of that year allowed commonties to be divided up between the proprietors, to enable enclosure and more modern forms of agriculture. However, the Act excluded commonties held by royal burghs or those in which royal burghs held servitudes.

There was widespread division and sale of commonties – often as a result of corrupt and self-interested landowners – during the nineteenth century. This gave rise to a number of cases, the most pertinent of which for present purposes is *Home v Young*[11], a case concerning a well and bleaching green in the village of Eyemouth. In that case, the land in question had been divided up under an action of division of commonty in 1764.

However, in a pivotal decision, the court held that tenants in the village of Eyemouth had customary rights to use the well and bleaching green as inhabitants of the burgh of barony of Eyemouth – irrespective of the commonty having been divided amongst the landowners, and all the proprietors consenting to Home's exclusive use of the ground. The baron was no more able to deprive the inhabitants of this privilege than he would have been able to close off the streets of the village[12].

Any "commonty" which is located in a former burgh can probably be safely treated as being part of the common good of that burgh. Conversely, however, the existence of a commonty in a small village or hamlet without any other evidence of incorporation into a burgh by way of charter does not necessarily imply the existence of a burgh but may only indicate rights in common or pertinents which can best be approached using the normal tools of property law[13].

As the reader will gather, the exact status of a particular settlement and implications for land or property located within it may not always be completely straightforward. Some assistance is given

---

11 (1846) 9 D 286. See also *Thorburn v Charters* (1841) 4 D 169.

12 See also **4.2** for development of the doctrine of customary rights generally.

13 If there is no incorporation of a burgh, the inhabitants are unable to claim the same rights of use: see *Henderson v Earl of Minto* (1860) 22 D 1126.

by more recent legislation. The Local Government (Scotland) Act 1947 attempted, not for the first time, to bring some semblance of order to the administration of local government in towns and cities. The First Schedule to the Act identified twenty-one large burghs, 176 small burghs and, in addition, Glasgow, Edinburgh, Aberdeen and Dundee, which were referred to for the purposes of that Act as "counties of cities". Appendix I reproduces the First Schedule to the 1947 Act. Whilst this is not necessarily a definitive list of settlements bearing common good, it certainly serves as a useful starting-point.

1.3   Burgh boundaries

As the years wear on from the time when burghs were actual live functioning, administrative units, it can sometimes become difficult to establish not only what was and was not a burgh, but also its actual extent. This is not so much to nail down the extent of its landholding. For one thing, the reader need look no further than the *Ruthin Castle* case to see that burghs could own land outwith their own boundaries. That case is discussed in much more detail in chapter 5 but, for now, it is necessary to look only briefly at the facts.

In November 1907, the late Duke of Fife disponed to the provost, magistrates and councillors of the Royal Burgh of Banff and the provost, magistrates and councillors of the Burgh of MacDuff the estate of Duff House in the County of Banff which lay between the two burghs, although technically some of the estate was within the Banff burgh boundary (and none of it in MacDuff.) As will be seen, the property was held to fall *pro indiviso* into each burgh's common good[14].

There are two main reasons now for establishing the boundaries of the former burgh as opposed to the boundaries of any particular grant of land. First, it will establish those inhabitants whose interests the authority should have regard to when deciding how to deal

14 *Magistrates of Banff v Ruthin Castle Ltd* 1944 SC 36, 1944 SLT 373. See also the "servitude" cases, such as *Magistrates of Earlsferry v Malcolm* (1829) 7 S 755, (1832) 11 S 74.

with the common good generally. Secondly, if disbursements are being made from the common good fund only to inhabitants of the former burgh (as is usually the case) it is important to establish where that burgh was exactly and its limits.

Most burgh boundaries will have changed over the centuries. However, the intentions of Parliament when it enacted the legislation in 1973 transferring the common good to the district councils seem clear. It wanted the common good to be protected for the interests of the inhabitants of the then burgh. It follows on from that that the burgh boundaries delineated in 1973 should serve as the burgh boundaries for the purposes described above – despite what differences there might be to them historically. A good source for finding out where those boundaries were is the ordnance survey map edition which is closest to 1973[15].

1.4   Benefactors – common good and trusts

One issue best dealt with in the historical context of this chapter is the relationship between dispositions by benefactors into the common good and trusts. It is very easy to see how confusion could arise in this area, particularly in relation to later grants of common good land by benefactors. The word "trust" is liberally sprinkled over conveyances of common good land and property.

An example can be found in a disposition by the Duke of Hamilton to the town council of the Burgh of Hamilton. In this deed, the words of conveyance themselves do not include the word "trust". Instead, they refer to the provost, magistrates and town council of the Burgh of Hamilton as "representing the community of the said burgh and their successors in office for behoof of the whole body and community of the burgh". However, condition (THIRD) in the disposition states that the subjects "shall be held in trust always for behoof of and solely for the use, recreation and enjoyment of the inhabitants of the Burgh of Hamilton and shall be used as a public park or recreation ground only".

---

15 See the available resources on the internet, such as http://geo.nls.uk/ indexes/info.html.

In other deeds, for example the disposition in favour of the Burgh of Leven of King George's Field in Leven, Fife, the words of conveyance themselves refer to the subjects being disponed to the burgh "as trustees for the inhabitants of the Burgh of Leven and the public generally for the purposes hereinafter specified". Condition (FIRST) in that deed then states that the subjects are dedicated "[as a King George's field] and they shall be held by us and our foresaids as trustees foresaid in all time coming for the purpose of a playing field for public recreation for behoof of the inhabitants of the Burgh of Leven and public generally".

There are many other examples that could be drawn from common good titles across the country. The magic phrase "trustees for behoof of the community" tends to crop up with regularity although not always in the same place or places in the deed. What exactly does that phrase mean? Were the subjects of these deeds intended to be held in a public trust by the magistrates for the community? Or is the word "trust", then as now, used in a looser sense than the strict legal definition?

"Trust" has a very appealing ring to it. Nowadays, many organisations of the great and good designate themselves as a "trust", whether their actual constitution is an unincorporated association, a company limited by guarantee or a trust in the proper legal sense. Do these old titles show the same desire for public confidence rather than a specific juridical intention?

The first common good case to deal with this in detail was that of *Provost, Magistrates and Councillors of Banff v Ruthin Castle Ltd*[16]. In this case, the disponer, the Duke of Fife, made a gift of the estate of Duff House to the burghs of Banff and MacDuff jointly "and to their joint assignees". The wording of the deed itself did not make any mention of "trust". However, the two burgh councils, acting jointly as a separate body known as Duff House Trustees, administered the estate on behalf of the two burghs.

The full facts of the case and its implications are set out later on in chapter 5, and have already been touched on in **1.3**. For now, it can again be noted that the case concerned whether or not Duff

---

16 *Magistrates of Banff v Ruthin Castle Ltd* 1944 SC 36, 1944 SLT 373.

House fell into the common good of both burghs jointly, or whether it was, in effect, a separate piece of trust estate set up by the disposition.

The court held that no trust had been created. Apart from the lack of use of the word "trust", it was clear that there was a lack of intention on the part of the Duke of Fife to do anything other than give a free gift of the property. There were no separate trustees and beneficiaries as would be required legally to create a trust, the town councils holding the property in the name of the beneficiary communities. Lastly, no trust purposes had been delineated in the deed or anything that could be said to be trust purposes.

A similar result was achieved in the case of *McDougall's Trustees v HM Advocate*[17]. Mr McDougall wanted to give the City of Edinburgh a public park and bought the property by obtaining a loan from the common good of the city to cover the purchase price and expenses of the purchase. The property was then conveyed by the sellers with the consent of Mr McDougall to the council as representing the community of the city. There was a condition restricting the use of the subjects to a park which was declared to be a real burden. There was also the usual irritancy clause. The Lord Justice-Clerk, in finding that no separate trust existed and that therefore the debt to the common good could be discounted for estate duty purposes, found that the restriction on use was an ordinary real burden as opposed to a trust purpose.

Frustratingly, the next reported case which dealt with this issue in any depth did not refer to a deed which used the magic word trust either. This was *Wilson v Inverclyde Council*[18]. A feu contract of 1772 had vested the harbour in the burgh of Greenock. Mr Wilson sought a declarator against the local authority that a public trust had been created by that feu contract, that it was currently lawful and active and that the local authority was the statutory trustee by virtue of succeeding documents and Acts of Parliament and that he, as a resident of Greenock and taxpayer, was a beneficiary of the trust. The court refused the petition for declarator.

17 1952 SC 260.
18 2003 SC 366, 2004 SLT 265.

There was no effective separation of the legal title from the beneficial interests; in other words, the trustees and the beneficiaries were the same. Again, there were no distinctive trust purposes.

Lastly, there is the case of *South Lanarkshire Council, Petitioners*[19]. Although this case is not strong authority on any point, because of the circumstances of disposal as outlined in chapter 6, the process includes a very well-reasoned argument by Professor Robert Rennie as to why the property in question falls into the common good of the former burgh of Hamilton instead of being a public trust – even though the magic words are used in the deed of conveyance to the burgh.

The narrative clause contains a desire on the part of the Duke of Hamilton to convey the subjects "for the purpose of being held and administered by them in trust as a public park for the benefit of the inhabitants of the said burgh". There is a condition to the same effect amongst the burdens clause as well as the usual irritancy clause. Professor Rennie in his Opinion deals with the authorities mentioned above and then advises that the deed does not create a public trust because, taking the deed as a whole, it is a conveyance and not a trust deed. He makes specific mention of the fact that the words of conveyance do not mention a trust element and the rest of the wording of the deed, and in particular the presence of an irritancy clause, suggest that it is a conveyance to the burgh and not a trust deed.

The truth is that the use of the word "trust" derives in the main part from a desire on the part of the granters of such deeds to reflect the nature of the relationship between the magistrates and the community in the management of the property gifted. It reflects some of the judicial reasoning in mid-nineteenth century cases as judges wrestled with a way of describing the exercise of customary rights by the community by means of analogy to existing juridical tools[20]. However, that does not of itself create a trust.

This leaves open the question of whether a disposition which uses the magic word "trust" in the words of conveyance – several

---

19 Inner House, 11 August 2004, unreported.
20 See the discussion of this point at **4.2**.

of which exist – would get closer to creating a public trust. Such an inference should be resisted wherever possible. The argument that Professor Rennie mentions in the earlier cases of the trustees and the beneficiaries being one and the same is particularly persuasive, whether or not the word trust is used in the words of conveyance. He seems to hit upon the true reason for using the word in deeds of this nature when he states that it is used as a "prohibition of alienation". Lastly, even if the word trust is used throughout, it would be difficult to establish in most deeds exactly what the trust purposes were and whether they could be said still to exist[21].

For these reasons, suggestions that deeds of this nature create a public trust should be resisted wherever possible, in favour of an interpretation of the properties falling into the common good of the former burgh concerned. Apart from anything else, all parties are then in a slightly clearer place as regards alienation of such property. Life, in short, is complicated enough with common good without the additional complications of trust law intruding.

As mentioned in the preface, common good law is principally an area dominated by principles derived from case law. However, there is a statutory framework of sorts. Turning to this next will give an understanding of how legislation both modern and otherwise has shaped, and in some instances been shaped by, that case law.

---

21 But for a non-common good example of a successful argument that a public trust had been created, see *Renouf's Trustees v Haining* 1919 SC 497.

Chapter 2

Statutory framework

2.1 Earlier statutory controls

Very early statutory controls, such as the Common Good Act 1491 (partly repealed), appear to have fallen into desuetude from the eighteenth century on. Nineteenth-century case law relies instead on the institutional writers such as Erskine, and previous decisions.

At the close of the nineteenth century, the common good of burghs started to come under stricter statutory control. Part of the policy behind this was the disposal/alienation of land issue and, in particular, a string of cases examined in more detail shortly such as *Sanderson v Lees*[1]; *Grahame v Magistrates of Kirkcaldy*[2]; *Paterson v Magistrates of St Andrews*[3]; *Blackie v Magistrates of Edinburgh*[4]; and, in particular, the Inner House decision in *Murray v Magistrates of Forfar*[5] in 1893, which set out quite clear guidelines on what might, and might not, be alienated from the common good of a burgh.

Another issue, however, was the increasing desire of ratepayers to see how the finances of their burgh were being administered. Sundry bits of legislation had created something of a patchwork quilt of regulatory authorities. As well as increased professional-isation of bodies such as the police, new utilities such as gas and sewerage systems had to be installed and regulated. Public health had also become a major issue as the Victorians began to master

1 (1859) 22 D 24.
2 (1879) 6 R 1066.
3 (1880) 7 R 712, (1881) 8 R (HL) 117.
4 (1884) 11 R 783.
5 (1893) 20 R 908, (1893) 1 SLT 105.

ways of overcoming – or at least controlling – the infectious diseases that had previously caused widespread pandemics.

The Town Councils (Scotland) Act 1900 attempted to deal with all these issues. Section 8 vested all matters under the Burgh Police (Scotland) Act 1892 and any bodies of police, gas or water commissioners which were town councils under another name in the town councils themselves. Section 9 took the consolidation process further by ensuring that a town council could sue and be sued in its corporate name and that title to all lands acquired by the town council was to be taken in its name, as well as execution of all deeds, contracts and "writs of importance" being granted in the corporate name.

So far as the keeping of accounts was concerned, sections 91 to 96 required councils to submit to audit requirements under the scrutiny of the Secretary for Scotland. In particular, section 92 required the council to make out an account

"of all the monies received and expended by them on account of the common good and revenue of the burgh, and on account of any rates or assessments levied or collected, or money realised, received, or borrowed by them under the Burgh Police (Scotland) Act, 1892, or any other Act under which they are authorised to levy assessments or uplift or borrow money."

Section 93 required that the account be made out "so as to exhibit a complete state, showing the common good and all other assets, and also the liabilities of the burgh".

A separate provision in section 97 dealt with the keeping of accounts in relation to any "charity, foundation or mortification". Similar audit requirements applied.

The last few paragraphs might seem to be delving into a rather uninteresting set of statutory provisions which are little more than historical curiosities. However, these sections are crucial to the understanding of some key case law scrutinised in chapter 5. The burgh had evolved from its mediaeval forebears. It might receive some income from petty customs, harbour dues, etc in terms of its original burgh charter, but its main source of income was, in fact, rating assessments raised under more recent legislation. Land might have been appropriated in terms of the original burgh charter or later additions by specific grant for community purposes. However, it could also now be acquired for statutory purposes – for road widening, for example, under the Burgh Police (Scotland) Act 1892[6].

So far as disposal of heritable property was concerned, section 98 provided that all "feus, alienations, or tacks [leases] for more than five years, of any heritable property of the burgh, or vested in the Council, so far as forming part of the common good" had to proceed by way of public roup (auction). Public notice had to be given by advertisements published once weekly for at least three weeks immediately preceding the day of roup in a local newspaper on pain of any such "feus, alienations, leases[7] or tacks" being void and null.

At first blush, section 98 seems to give carte blanche to town councils to sell any common good land, completely superseding the earlier common law position. However, the next major common good case, *Magistrates of Kirkcaldy v Marks & Spencer Ltd*[8] was not contested on this basis. Instead, both parties to the case seemed to have accepted that section 98 was subject to the common law rule that some common good properties were not capable of alienation.

What happened in the case was this. The magistrates of Kirkcaldy had decided that new municipal buildings were required. On 13 May 1935, they resolved to sell the existing town hall and adjoining property, located at the corner of High Street and Tolbooth Street, some of which formed part of what was described as "the old commonty". Whilst waiting for the new municipal buildings to be erected, the civic functions of the council and its committees were transferred to other buildings – in particular, the meetings of the council and its committees were held in police buildings which had been opened in 1903.

---

6 Section 154. And various other purposes: see **5.3**.
7 "Lease" is not mentioned in the earlier part of the section and it is not clear why it appears here given that it is synonymous with tack.
8 1937 SLT 574.

This accommodation was better for meetings than the old town house[9].

The former town house and associated buildings were then sold to Marks & Spencer, having followed the procedure for public roup and advertisement in terms of the 1900 Act. However, at some point after a contract was concluded, Marks & Spencer became concerned as to the ability of the town council to alienate the town buildings and refused to implement the articles of roup and sale between them and the council.

In the Outer House, Lord Jamieson, whilst noting that the subjects had been properly advertised in terms of the 1900 Act, took no further notice of it and proceeded to decide the case on the basis of the old authorities about alienability. Following Lord Pitmilly in *Phin v Magistrates of Auchtermuchty*[10], he found that the general rule was that buildings which were essential to the performance of the burgh's functions could not be alienated normally. However, in this case, he found a way of distinguishing the earlier authority, stating:

> "It cannot be said that to hold the Council meetings in the Burgh Court, which is the property of the burgh, until new municipal buildings are erected will lead either to inefficient administration of public business or in any way detract from the dignity of the burgh. In these circumstances, I am of opinion that the subjects advertised for sale were not inalienable and that the pursuers were entitled to sell them and are in a position to give a good title."[11]

The replacement town house referred to in the case is still in use as a local government office and is the building referred to in the preface. Marks & Spencer went ahead with the development of the corner of High Street and Tolbooth Street and can still be found

---

9 This had itself been the subject of an earlier case, reported as *Magistrates of Kirkcaldy, Petitioners* (1826) 4 S 547, in which the magistrates presented a petition, asking consent of the court to move their place of meeting. The laconic report says: "The Court being of Opinion that no such application was necessary, and that it might be productive of injurious consequences to give any sanction to it, refused it as unnecessary."

10 (1827) 5 S 690.

11 1937 SLT at 577.

in the High Street[12]. However, the case was to have one last twist
to it – in the shape of the next set of statutory provisions.

This was the Local Government (Scotland) Act 1947. William
Hutton, in his annotated version of the Act, describes it as "an
excellent example of the simplification and clarification of the law
that results from consolidation"[13]. Hutton points out that, in 382
sections and fourteen Schedules, the law "scattered over the statute
book of the last 120 years" in 178 separate enactments was brought
together in a single piece of legislation.

Part IX of the Act provided for a single burgh fund for all the
various types of receipts and expenditure now received and payable
by a burgh council for such things as housing, roads, water, etc.
Section 180 excluded, otherwise than by resolution of the council,
the common good fund from that burgh fund, effectively ousting
the common good fund from its historical position as the central
fund for the burgh administration. The common good was being
marginalised by the increased statutory powers and responsibilities
of mid-twentieth century local authorities. There were other provisions relating to uses of common good monies which are no
longer relevant.

There were also provisions[14] allowing for creation of small
burghs, or for them to be dissolved and their area to form part of
the landward area of a county council. Section 134(5) provided that
any agreement to dissolve a burgh should make provision with respect to the property and liabilities of the burgh "including any
relating to the common good of the burgh". The writer is not aware
of any burgh having been dissolved in this way but, if they had been,
this would not necessarily mean that common good properties
formerly held by that burgh would have disappeared altogether.

The main provisions which are still of interest for the purposes
of understanding the case law, however, lie in section 171, relating
to the disposal of property.

The relevant section dealing with common good property dis-

---

12 The current town house was not, in fact, completed until 1947 because of
    the onset of war.
13 William Hutton, *The Local Government (Scotland) Act 1947* (1949) at p 1 of
    the preface.
14 Sections 133 and 134.

posals, section 171, comes as part of a package of measures forming Part VIII of the Act dealing with acquisition of and dealings in land by local authorities. This was 1947, and the authorities – particularly in the cities – were involved in large-scale slum clearance, completion of environmental improvements that the Luftwaffe had initiated, and the provision of large-scale social rented housing. The provisions in general freed up the ability of local authorities to acquire and dispose of land and tied in with the partial modernisation of the compulsory acquisition legislation by means of the Acquisition of Land (Authorisation Procedure) (Scotland) Act 1947[15].

Before looking at section 171, it is worth noting section 162, not so much for its terms – which essentially repeated the 1900 Act by stating that the title to all land acquired by a local authority shall be taken in the corporate name of the authority – but for the annotation to the provision by Hutton in his commentary on the Act[16]. Hutton comments that a practice had grown up of title being taken in the name of, for example, "the Town Council of the Burgh of Y, as local authority under the Housing (Scotland) Acts 1925 to 1946". Hutton commends the practitioner to adopt this practice rather than simply quoting the corporate name of the authority as "a purchaser or feuar from the local authority is entitled to know the purpose for which the land was acquired so that he may know the powers of the local authority in regard to its disposal and to have evidence of any consents required". As will be seen, that commentary has particular relevance for what is, and is not, held within the common good[17].

Section 171, which dealt with the disposal of land, fell into four subsections.

The first subsection said that the general principles relating to "the appropriation, letting, selling, feuing, or excambing of land belonging to a local authority and the application of capital monies

15 As regards compulsory purchase, there is tentative authority for the rights of the inhabitants requiring separate acquisition under compulsory purchase order, although the bench did express "perplexity": see *Cunningham v Edinburgh and Northern Railway Co* (1847) 9 D 1469.

16 Hutton, p 265.

17 See **5.4**.

received in respect of land" were to apply to land forming part of the common good of a burgh "with respect to which land no question arises as to the right of the Town Council to alienate". In other words, if no question arose as to the ability of the authority to sell the common good land, then the rest of the provisions of the Act would apply.

Subsection (2) allowed a town council, with the consent of the Secretary of State, to sell or feu common good land or the buildings on it

> "where such land or the buildings thereon have at some time been used as a town hall or offices or buildings for the transaction of the business of the burgh and have ceased or are about to cease to be so used, notwithstanding any question as to right of the council to alienate such land or buildings".

Mr Hutton, who was to provide the commentary on the Act, and who seems to have been closely associated with the committee that produced the draft proposals for the legislation, had had his revenge. He had been the town clerk of Kirkcaldy at the time of *Magistrates of Kirkcaldy v Marks & Spencer*. The very case which had troubled his council – and the Court of Session – before was now to be dealt with effectively under the delegated powers by the Secretary of State.

Subsection (3) allowed authorities to dispose of land forming part of the common good which was not excepted under the previous subsections (ie, those properties where a question arose and they were not municipal buildings) to go to the Court of Session or the sheriff for authority to sell or feu it.

Lastly, subsection (4) allowed the Secretary of State under subsection (2), or the Court of Session or the sheriff under subsection (3), to require the town council to provide substitute land for that which was being sold.

Clearly, the new regime relating to disposal of common good land was much more sophisticated than its predecessor of the 1900 Act. And although what might be called the Kirkcaldy clause was to disappear when the 1947 Act was repealed by the Local Government (Scotland) Act 1973, otherwise many of the problems still troubling lawyers in the current legislation

were put in place in the immediate aftermath of the Second
World War.

2.2   The Local Government (Scotland) Act 1973

The 1973 Act marked a watershed in the administration of local
government in Scotland. After a century and a half of tinkering
about, central government finally abolished the burghs, as well as
the elaborate system of county councils, district councils and so on
that had been set up around them. Instead, a relatively simple
system of two-tier government in most areas was brought in, con-
sisting of district and regional councils. The exceptions were
Orkney, Shetland and the Western Isles where islands councils
operated as a unitary authority.

Yet despite these sweeping changes, the problem of the common
good remained. Section 222(2) provided for the Secretary of State
to transfer property held as part of the common good to islands
or district councils as specified by order and that those councils –
other than the four main cities – were, in administering that property, to "have regard to the interests of the inhabitants of the area
to which the common good formerly related". Section 222(3) dealt
with Aberdeen, Dundee, Edinburgh and Glasgow by requiring the
district councils of those cities to have regard to the interests of all
the inhabitants of their districts, presumably the thinking being that
the cities were more or less coterminous with the original burghs.
The Local Authorities (Property etc) (Scotland) Order 1975[18] so
provided in article 10.

As an aside, it is worth noting that there may be properties that
could be said to form part of the common good which did not transfer to the district councils under section 222(2) and its attendant
property order. These might include, for example, former reservoirs
of burghs previously transferred to water boards and now in the
hands of Scottish Water via the regional councils, and harbours,
which were a functional responsibility of the regional councils. In
the event of a dispute over these properties now, the wording of
the relevant property orders would need close interpretation.

18 SI 1975/659.

However, the main problem left to be dealt with was what to
do with disposal of common good land. There did not appear to
have been a lot of reported authorities between 1947 and 1973 and
this seems to have encouraged the legislators to keep the provisions
relating to disposal of common good land, as also the other acquisition and disposal measures in which the provisions nested, pretty
much the same. As previously stated, the "Kirkcaldy exemption"
relating to the disposal of former town hall buildings being determined by the Minister disappeared. Section 75 reads:

> **"75. Disposal, etc, of land forming part of the common
> good**
>
> (1) The provisions of this Part of this Act with respect to the
>   appropriation or disposal of land belonging to a local authority
>   shall apply in the case of land forming part of the common
>   good of an authority with respect to which land no question
>   arises as to the right of the authority to alienate.
>
> (2) Where a local authority desire to dispose of land forming
>   part of the common good with respect to which land a
>   question arises as to the right of the authority to alienate,
>   they may apply to the Court of Session or the Sheriff to
>   authorise them to dispose of the land, and the Court or
>   Sheriff may, if they think fit, authorise the authority to dis-
>   pose of the land subject to such conditions, if any, as they may
>   impose, and the authority shall be entitled to dispose of land
>   accordingly.
>
> (3) The Court of Session or Sheriff acting under subsection (2)
>   above may impose a condition requiring that the local auth-
>   ority shall provide in substitution for the land proposed to be
>   disposed of other land to be used for the same purpose for
>   which the former land was used."

As has been noted, the provision relating to disposal of common
good land is nested in a larger set of provisions dealing inter alia
with acquisition of land by agreement, acquisition of land compul-
sorily, appropriation of land and disposal of land. The effect of the
wording of section 75(1) is to enable a local authority to appropriate land into the common good – but not to acquire it for a
common good purpose. This might be a possibility where replacement land is being provided for common good land which is being
sold, or even for some other reason. It is, therefore, at least theo-

retically possible for a local authority to increase its common good land holding even now, over twenty years after the burghs ceased to exist[19].

Similarly, the provisions of section 74 regarding disposal of land are held to apply to common good land where no question arises as to the right of the authority to alienate that land. Section 74(1) allows a local authority to dispose of land held by it in any manner it wishes except that (section 74(2)) without the consent of the Scottish Ministers, it cannot dispose of land for a consideration which is less than the best that can reasonably be obtained. Section 74(2) has been amended by the Local Government in Scotland Act 2003, section 11, subject to further regulations which are still awaited at the time of writing. Thus, where no question arises as to the right of an authority to alienate common good land, it is disposed of under the same statutory scheme introduced by section 74 and commented on in cases such as *Stannifer Ltd v Glasgow Development Agency*[20].

It is worth noting that section 74 does not actually apply to land forming part of the common good where a question does arise as to the ability of the authority to alienate. This means that, in theory, if such a piece of land is to be disposed of and the sheriff or the Court of Session consents to it without imposing conditions, the local authority could sell it off without having regard to best consideration principles as outlined in section 74. However, remembering the requirements in section 222(2) and (3) that the property has to be administered with a regard being had to the interests of all the inhabitants of the former burghs (or the new district council areas of the cities), this minor point is probably of little practical importance. Having regard to the best interests of the burgh residents appears to put the same or similar obligation on the local authority to obtain the best consideration that could reasonably be obtained in disposals.

After many years and many legislative reforms, therefore, and despite subsequent legislation to be explored next, the main statutory framework for common good law relates only to the disposal

19 See also the discussion of appropriation, alienation and disposal in **6.1**.
20 1999 SC 156.

of common good property and is found in section 75 of the Local Government (Scotland) Act 1973. In that context, it is unfortunate that the provisions of section 75 only seem to obfuscate common good law even more than was previously the case. In particular, what does section 75(1) mean when it talks about land being land where "no question arises as to the right of the authority to alienate?" Does the word "disposal" mean exactly the same as the word "alienation" in this context? And what criteria should the court apply to determine whether or not the disposal should take place and under what conditions if a question does arise?

These points deserve fuller explanation along with the unanswered questions the common law throws up in the following few chapters. However, in the meantime, it is useful to look at how the 1973 Act's provisions interact with later pieces of legislation.

2.3   Interaction of 1973 Act with later legislation

Apart from a minor mention in paragraph 30, Schedule 3 to the Local Government (Scotland) Act 1975, which excepts borrowing on the security of the common good from certain requirements relating to a local authority's borrowing generally, there is very little further statutory mention of the common good until the Local Government etc (Scotland) Act 1994. This Act reorganised local government completely less than twenty years on from the 1973 Act, creating a system of unitary authorities throughout Scotland. However, the provisions relating to common good did little other than transfer on responsibility for common good property to the newer authorities. Section 15(4) provided for the onward transfer and repeated the provision that, in administering such property, any authority to which it was transferred was to have regard to the interests of the "inhabitants of the area to which the common good related prior to 16 May 1975", the formal date of extinction of the burghs (except in the cases of Aberdeen, Dundee, Edinburgh and Glasgow, which were to have regard to the interests of all the inhabitants of their areas, for the reasons discussed above). It is perhaps worth noting that sections 16 and 17 respectively dealt separately with property held on trust and educational endowments, increasing the presumption that property can either be held on the common good or held on trust but not both[21].

In due course, the Local Authorities (Property Transfer) (Scotland) Order 1995[22] arranged for transfer on of common good property to the new authorities. A search of the phrase "common good" in the usual databases throws up very few other references to it and even fewer which are of any real relevance. However, there is one other statute which specifically mentions common good, which predates the 1994 Act and is worthy of mention, and that is the Tenants' Rights (Scotland) Act 1980.

The Tenants' Rights (Scotland) Act 1980 first introduced the right to buy for council house tenants. The legislation was extended and codified in the Housing (Scotland) Act 1987. However, what if the council house were to form part of the common good?

This was not as unusual as it might seem. Old burgh chambers and the like had often had associated accommodation for civic functionaries who had long departed leaving the accommodation to be taken over by council tenants. In public parks and so on, properties which might originally have been used under "tied tenancies" for the accommodation of park keepers, etc, had become subject to secure tenancies[23]. If these properties formed part of a common good title which made them inalienable, how did this square with the right-to-buy legislation?

Fortunately, the Tenants' Rights (Scotland) Act 1980[24] more or less clears up the mystery by making it clear that the right-to-buy provisions include tenancies of properties forming part of the common good. This could be said to put the issue beyond doubt although, even if that provision did not exist, the 1973 Act provisions would probably mean that any council house subject to

21 See **1.4**.
22 SI 1995/2499.
23 There is a string of cases dealing with this issue, eg: *Smith v Dundee City Council* 2001 Hous LR 78; *Hughes v Greenwich London Borough Council* [1994] 1 AC 170; *Docherty v City of Edinburgh Council* 1985 SLT (Lands Tr) 61; and *De Fontenay v Strathclyde Regional Council* 1990 SLT 605.
24 Section 1(10)(a), now Housing (Scotland) Act 1987, s 62(2)(a)(i).

right-to-buy provisions could be sold without the necessity of
going to court. Section 75 says only that the Court of Session or
the sheriff's consent to sale is required in relation to land in
respect of which "a question arises" of the ability of the council
to dispose of it. In the case of properties under right-to-buy provisions, the authority is actually legally obliged to sell the property to a secure tenant in terms of legislation which, of course,
is subsequent to the 1973 Act (and therefore will be presumed
by the general rule of law to supersede it where there is any
inconsistency).

So much for legislation which actually mentions the common
good. However, the statutory framework relating to common
good does not operate in a vacuum. The legislation subsequent to
the 1973 Act which has the most obvious impact perhaps is that
relating to feudal reform and the surprisingly limited impact of that
will be examined shortly. However, there are one or two other
pieces of legislation which are likely to have an impact on common
good land in particular.

The Land Reform (Scotland) Act 2003 contains a number of
far-reaching provisions, including, in Part 2, the community right
to buy. The community right to buy land is said to extend to
"registrable land" (section 33). This is described as any land other
than excluded land, being land as described as such in an Order
made by the Ministers (section 33(2)). Community bodies, as
described in section 34, have a right to register an interest in land
with the Keeper. This interest activates a right to buy (section 47)
where the owner of the land proposes to sell it. The community
body is then entitled to exercise its right to buy with the approval
of the community and the consent of Ministers (section 51). There
are provisions relating to a community ballot and ministerial
approval contained in Chapter 4 of the Act. Section 37 provides for
registration of an interest in the land. Chapter 5 of the Act makes
provision for valuation in such circumstances.

It is quite likely, given the sensitive nature of common good
land, that local communities may feel that the provisions of this
legislation should be applied to common good land. There is, on
the face of it, no reason why this legislation should not apply to
it.

Another post-1973 piece of legislation which might have a surprising effect on common good law is the Local Government in Scotland Act 2003. This piece of legislation, whilst not reforming the structure of local government itself, introduced three key themes of local government into legislative context: community planning, best value, and the power to advance well-being.

The interaction of the new best value regime with the common good funds is dealt with in chapter 3. In the meantime, there may be some interesting effects produced by sections 20 to 22 of the Local Government in Scotland Act 2003.

Section 20(1), in the type of sweeping statement that is so popular amongst legislative draftsmen nowadays, says:

> "A local authority has power to do anything which it considers is
> likely to promote or improve the well-being of –
> (a) its area and persons within that area; or
> (b) either of those."

This general dispensing provision is designed to change the culture of local government by allowing councils to take action unless, in the words of section 22(1), there is a "limiting provision" restricting the authority's powers. In the context of the common good and, in particular, in relation to the disposal of common good land, it would seem that section 75 of the 1973 Act constitutes a "limiting provision" in that it sets out exactly when an authority can dispose of common good land and when it cannot. However, the provision may have an effect on appropriations and alienations falling short of disposal, a topic examined in more detail in chapter 6.

2.4   Common good and burdens: impact of feudal reform

With the same legislative chutzpah as the Scotland Act 1998 announcing that there shall be a Scottish Parliament[25], the Abolition of Feudal Tenure etc (Scotland) Act 2000 has as its opening gambit:

---

25 Scotland Act 1998, s 1(1): 'There shall be a Scottish Parliament.'

"The feudal system of land tenure, that is to say the entire system whereby land is held by a vassal on perpetual tenure from a superior is, on the appointed day, abolished."

As every conveyancer in Scotland knows, the appointed day was 28 November 2004 when, along with the abolition of the feudal system, a new system of real burdens came in as a consequence of the 2000 Act and its partner pieces of legislation, the Title Conditions (Scotland) Act 2003 and the Tenements (Scotland) Act 2004[26]. It is somewhat ironic, however, that common good law, itself a relic of the same twelfth-century feudal system introduced by David I and his successors, should remain largely untouched.

Not completely untouched, however. Some common good funds may suffer a slight diminution in income as a result of extinction of feu duties previously payable to the common good on the appointed day[27]. In practice, this diminution of income will be fairly small, with a greater loss being redemption money payable on first sale after 1974[28]. Similarly, any feu duty payable out of the common good to a superior or even the Crown will have been extinguished as at the appointed day. The only exception to these rules would be if preservation notices had been served within two years after the appointed day[29].

The main effect on common good brought about by feudal reform will be in relation to titles to common good land. As already mentioned[30], many nineteenth-century and early twentieth-century dispositions of common good land were made by way of feudal grant, particularly where the superior wanted to impose burdens requiring the burgh to use the particular land or building for a particular purpose, such as a public park, museum and so on. In the absence of any successful attempt to preserve the burden under one or other of the relevant provisions of the 2000 Act – an

---

26 See the Abolition of Feudal Tenure etc (Scotland) Act 2000, ss 71 and 77 and the Title Conditions (Scotland) Act 2003, ss 122(1) and 129.
27 Abolition of Feudal Tenure etc (Scotland) Act 2000, s 7.
28 Land Tenure Reform (Scotland) Act 1974, s 24(2).
29 Abolition of Feudal Tenure etc (Scotland) Act 2000, s 8.
30 See **1.4**.

attempt that would in most instances be difficult to justify – the feudal burdens will now have no effect and will, in due course, be cleaned from the register by the Keeper[31].

But does this mean that the common good nature of a title has disappeared? Prior to feudal abolition, a cautious approach was often taken by authorities. The burden in the title expressing, for example, the requirement that the burgh use the land for a public park may have constituted a condition enforceable by the feudal superior. However, it also set up a quality of title which gave the title an inalienable nature. Where a common good property was to be sold, therefore, and a question arose as to its alienability, the safe approach appeared to be not just to take the matter to court under section 75 of the 1973 Act but also to obtain a minute of waiver from the feudal superior.

That second requirement will, of course, now disappear. There is, however, a practical difficulty in relation to feudal reform and common good titles of this kind and that is the disappearance from the register of certain burdens because they are no longer enforceable as feudal conditions. The only comfort here is that most of the titles in question will still subsist in the Register of Sasines and are unlikely to be affected by amendments to the Land Register.

For the sake of completeness, it is worth noting that some superiors in situations such as this might still have a right of enforcement as neighbour under the new legislation or as a matter of contract[32].

Having looked at the historical origins of the common good, regard has now been had to the statutory framework under which common good law operates. It is evident that the statutory treatment of common good itself is relatively light although other legislative reforms have left their mark in various ways. Before looking at how the common law answers some of the questions left unanswered by the statutory framework, however, the next chapter will look at how the common good is administered in practice.

31 Abolition of Feudal Tenure etc (Scotland) Act 2000, s 46.
32 For discussion of these matters, see K G C Reid, *The Abolition of Feudal Tenure in Scotland* (2004); and, in particular, para 2.6.

Chapter 3

The administration of the common good

3.1 Administration and delegation in local authorities

Chapter 2 showed how statutory provisions relating to the disposal of common good land nest amongst overall provisions relating to the acquisition, appropriation and disposal of local authority land generally[1]. In the same way, the law relating to the administration of the common good fund and any of its assets – scanty as it may be – is supplemented by the general law relating to the administration of local authority monies and assets. This might seem obvious. However, it is important to recognise that the requirement in local authorities to have regard to the inhabitants of the former burgh areas (or, in the case of the cities, all of the areas) does not stand alone[2]. Nor is it in some way fireproof against being affected by subsequent statutory provisions where these conflict with it.

Section 56 of the Local Government (Scotland) Act 1973 remains the basic foundation for how local authorities are administered. In terms of section 56, the local authority can arrange for the discharge of any of its functions by a committee, a sub-committee, an officer or (although this is extremely unlikely in the context of common good) another local authority in Scotland. However, each council is a body corporate[3] and, in theory, every decision of a council in relation to the discharge of its functions must trace back to an original decision of the council as a corporate body.

---

1 See **2.2**.
2 Local Government etc (Scotland) Act 1994, s 15(4).
3 Local Government etc (Scotland) Act 1994, s 2(3).

The practical effect of all of this theory, in most councils, is that the day-to-day decision-making function of the council is spread down through a system of committees and sub-committees to individual officers. Two key documents for this process are the scheme of administration – which sets out what functions are delegated from the full council down to committee and sub-committee level – and the scheme of delegation, which does the same for delegation to officers. A third is the set of standing orders which govern procedurally how decisions are made at committee.

In most councils, decisions relating to the common good are either taken by a specific common good committee or sub-committee, or by a property or policy and resources committee, particularly in relation to land disposal issues[4].

Decisions taken in relation to the common good, then, form the same pattern as other decision-making structures within local authorities. Day-to-day decisions are taken by officers on behalf of the council. Decisions outwith the ambit of the scheme of delegation, or perhaps decisions which will have important policy implications, are put to the relevant committee for decision.

Ultimately, all decisions and actions of the council – at least in theory – pass through the approval mechanism of the full council, although, in practice, the fine grain of some actions will not be picked up there.

What implications does this process have for people seeking to challenge a decision taken in relation to the common good? One way in which a challenge could be mounted would be by way of judicial review of a council decision. The Local Government in Scotland Act 2003, section 20, discussed above[5], weakens one of the legs of the *ultra vires* doctrine, by giving councils a general dispensing power to do anything which they consider will advance the well-being of the council area or its inhabitants. This will make it more difficult to argue that an authority was acting outwith its powers, in the purest sense. However, it does not remove that leg of the doctrine altogether.

4 See Appendix V.
5 See **2.3**.

See, for example, the recent case of *Standard Commercial Securities Ltd v Glasgow City Council*[6]. This case concerned the vexed question of what constituted the "best consideration" that a local authority could obtain in disposing of land. Section 191(3) of the Town and Country Planning (Scotland) Act 1997 requires a planning authority which has acquired or appropriated land for any planning purposes not to dispose of it for "otherwise than at the best price or on the best terms that can reasonably obtain". Subsection (10) provides that section 191 "shall have effect to the exclusion of provisions of any enactment, other than this Act, by virtue of or under which the planning authority are or may be authorised to dispose of land held by them".

The effect of the latter provision was to put beyond any doubt the inapplicability of the general dispensing power contained in section 20 of the Local Government in Scotland Act 2003. Accordingly, the old case law regarding the *vires* of a council's actions came back into play and, in this case, the court held that the council had not, in reaching a back-to-back agreement with the developer at the stage of the process it had, acted consistently with the provisions of section 191[7].

There are also two other legs to the *ultra vires* doctrine. The first of these is that a decision was taken or acted upon beyond the proper delegated authority of the decision-taker or actor – if, for example, an officer made a decision relating to the application of common good funds which was outwith any delegation made to that level by either the council's scheme of delegation or any specific committee decision. Internal procedures must be followed fairly closely.

---

6 2005 SLT 144 (IH); for the Outer House decision, see 2004 SLT 655. An
   earlier judicial review involving the same parties is reported at 2001 SC
   177.
7 Section 20 of the Local Government in Scotland Act 2003 is not, in fact,
   mentioned in the judgment. However, what is said in that case necessarily
   implies that the general dispensing power provided by the "power to
   advance well-being" was of no assistance given that s 191 was effectively a
   "limiting provision" for the purposes of s 21 of the 2003 Act. It is
   understood at time of writing that the case is under appeal to the House of
   Lords and will be heard in October 2006.

The other route open to an objector seeking to challenge a decision relating to a common good would be to claim that the decision was what has become known as "*Wednesbury* unreasonable". This well-known doctrine has its foundation in the case of *Associated Provincial Picture Houses Ltd v Wednesbury Corporation*[8]. In that case, the court upheld a condition attached to a permission for Sunday performances granted by a licensing authority to the effect that no children under the age of fifteen years would be admitted to any entertainment, whether accompanied by an adult or not.

The case is well known but it is perhaps worth quoting one of the landmark passages in Lord Greene's judgment to stress the very high test that is put on someone trying to claim a decision of a local authority was so unreasonable as to be *ultra vires*:

> "It is true the discretion must be exercised reasonably. Now what does that mean? Lawyers familiar with the phraseology commonly used in relation to exercise of statutory discretions often use the word "unreasonable" in a rather comprehensive sense. It has frequently been used and is frequently used as a general description of the things which must not be done. For instance, a person entrusted with a discretion must, so to speak, direct himself properly in law. He must call his own attention to the matters which he is bound to consider. He must exclude from his consideration matters which are irrelevant to what he has to consider. If he does not obey those rules, he may truly be said, and often is said, to be acting 'unreasonably'. Similarly, there may be something so absurd that no sensible person could ever dream that it lay within the powers of the authority. Warrington LJ in *Short v Poole Corporation* [[1926] Ch 66, 90, 91] gave the example of the red-haired teacher, dismissed because she had red hair. That is unreasonable in one sense. In another sense it is taking into consideration extraneous matters. It is so unreasonable that it might almost be described as being done in bad faith; and, in fact, all these things run into one another."

The concept of unreasonability was explored in the Scottish context in *Wordie Property Company Ltd v Secretary of State for Scotland*[9].

8 [1948] 1 KB 223.
9 1984 SLT 345.

That case concerned a comprehensive development area in central Aberdeen which was the subject of a compulsory purchase order. There were rival planning applications for redevelopment of all or part of the area, one of them from the Wordie Property Company. The rival applications were called in by the Secretary of State for determination along with the confirmation of the compulsory purchase order. After a six-week inquiry, Wordie's rival was granted planning permission and the compulsory purchase order was confirmed.

Lord Emslie, in his judgment[10], outlined the grounds on which an *ultra vires* application could be made:

> "A decision of the Secretary of State acting within the statutory remit is *ultra vires* if he has improperly exercised the discretion confided to him. In particular, it will be *ultra vires* if it is based upon a material error of law going to the root of the question for determination. It will be *ultra vires* too, if the Secretary of State has taken into account irrelevant considerations or has failed to take account of relevant and material considerations which ought to have been taken into account. Similarly, it will fall to be quashed on that ground if, where it is one for which a factual basis is required, there is no proper basis in fact to support it. It will also fall to be quashed if it, or any condition imposed in relation to a grant of planning permission, is so unreasonable that no reasonable Secretary of State could have reached or imposed it."

The court found that there was a real and substantial doubt as to what the reasons for the Secretary of State's decisions were and as to what matters he did or did not take into account, that the "essential factual foundation" for the reporter's report, which informed the Secretary of State's conclusions, was lacking and that the factual questions which had been dealt with in the wrong part of the reporter's report had been placed in the report in such a way that the appellants were prejudiced and that, therefore, the decisions of the Secretary of State fell to be quashed even though the decisions were not so unreasonable that no reasonable Secretary of State would have taken them.

10 At 347–348.

The area of judicial review is a large and constantly evolving area of the law in itself, and in a work of this length there seems little point in doing more than mentioning some of the leading authorities as a means of outlining the type of issues that a local authority has to consider in coming to a decision on matters relating to the common good – as it does for any other administrative decision.

To summarise these, an authority must take all relevant matters into consideration and disregard any irrelevant matters. It must have regard both to the external law and its own internal procedures and follow them both. The decision it takes must be founded upon some reasonable interpretation of factual reality. The authority's reasons for coming to the decision must be made plain or, at the very least, be capable of being deduced from the accompanying papers surrounding the decision. Lastly, the decision should not be so unreasonable that no reasonable authority would come to that decision.

Recent case law has made it plain that the courts will not be tremendously willing to intervene in an administrative decision of a local authority[11]. In the common good context, for example, a court would be very unlikely to interfere with a decision unless, for example, the interests of the inhabitants of the former burgh were disregarded entirely. That might be difficult to establish.

One of the more recent common good cases does, in fact, give some pointers as to how the court might deal with judicial review in a common good context. In *Cockenzie and Port Seton Community Council v East Lothian District Council*[12], the case had actually been brought by the community council as a judicial review of the district council's decision to demolish the Pond Hall, Port Seton. Its counsel argued that to do so would be *ultra vires* in the technical sense of being outwith the powers of the district council unless it had first proceeded to get the Secretary of State's consent in terms of section 75 of the 1973 Act. That argument failed because, essentially, Lord Osborne held that if the matter had come to him by way of an application under section 75 by the local authority, he

11 See, eg, *R (City of Westminster) v Mayor of London* [2002] EWHC 2240.
12 1997 SLT 81.

would have held that the common good property was capable of disposal, following the *Magistrates of Kirkcaldy v Marks & Spencer Ltd*[13] doctrine of there being a replacement building that fulfilled the same function.

More tellingly, counsel for the community council attempted to argue that the decision to proceed without reference to the court was *Wednesbury* unreasonable. This argument appears to have been introduced at a late stage and Lord Osborne gave it fairly short shrift. He said[14]:

> "[I]t does not appear to me to follow from the existence of [section 75 of the 1973 Act] that a local authority is bound to take that course. If a local authority desire to dispose of land forming part of the common good, with respect to which land a question arises as to the right of the authority to alienate, it appears to me that that local authority may, if they think fit, no doubt after having taken appropriate advice, proceed upon a view which commends itself to them to the effect that they have the right to alienate. In the event of their doing that, they are, of course, exposed to the risk that others may take the view that they do not possess the right to alienate. In that event, proceedings such as these proceedings may be brought against them."

At least in the context of disposal of common good land and the decision whether or not to refer the matter to court, this appears to be strong authority against arguments of *Wednesbury* unreasonability as being a ground of the authority's actings being *ultra vires*.

3.2   Common good and community councils

The 1973 reorganisation abolished burgh councils for good. In so doing, larger authorities were created and the Wheatley Commission Report[15] which informed the drafting of the legislation recog-

---

13 1937 SLT 574.

14 1997 SLT at 90.

15 Report of the Royal Commission on Local Government in Scotland, Cmnd 4150 (1969).

nised that local authorities might become distant from local issues. For this reason, Part IV of the 1973 Act provided for the establishment of community councils.

Part IV of the 1973 Act comprises sections 51 to 55 inclusive, of which section 54 has now been repealed. Briefly, section 51 provides for the establishment and general purpose of community councils; section 52 entrusts to local authorities the promotion of schemes for the creation of community councils, with section 53 providing for amendment of such schemes. Section 55 provides for assistance of certain kinds to be given by local authorities to community councils and that provision is now probably supplemented by section 20 of the Local Government in Scotland Act 2003[16].

Community councils have not been uniformly implemented since the 1973 Act. An early commentator on their operation said:

> "In practice, community councils have met with very differing degrees of success in different areas. It was never intended that they should form a third tier of local authority. They were therefore given no specific powers and duties. They have no right to levy rates or demand a share of the rates from their respective authorities. As a result, they are largely dependent on the generosity of their local authorities and this has varied from one area to another."[17]

Section 52 of the Local Government etc (Scotland) Act 1994 transfers the responsibility for the making of schemes for the establishment of community councils to the new unitary authorities and there are additional provisions regarding consultation in the event of such a scheme being made. However, nowhere in either Act is there any direct link between community councils and the common good. The common good is a statutory responsibility of the local authorities: between 1975 and 1996, islands and district councils, and now the unitary authorities. In administering the common good, local authorities are not required by statute to have regard to the views of community councils. They do have to have regard

---

16   See **2.3**.
17   K Ferguson, *An Introduction to Local Government in Scotland* (1984) at 41.

to the interests of the inhabitants of the former burghs (or in the case of the cities, the cities).

Why then have community councils come to see the common good as "theirs" in a way that suggests that they have a statutory right to direct the use of the funds?

Partly, the answer lies in geography. Many of the former burghs now host some of the most active community councils and there is a strong sense of identification between the former burgh councils and the current community councils. There are similarities in the boundaries of the former burghs and that of some community councils. Indeed, some retired politicians from the former have found their way onto the latter.

There is also backing for the community council's role in relation to common good in the original wording of the 1973 Act. Section 51(2) states the general purpose of a community council as being:

> "to ascertain, co-ordinate and express to the local authorities for its area, and to public authorities, the views of the community which it represents, in relation to matters for which these authorities are responsible, and to take such action in the interests of that community as appears to it to be expedient and practicable."

Prior to 1997, the law relating to title and interest was, to say the least, unhelpful to community councils wishing to challenge the actings of local authorities in relation to the common good through the courts. In *Conn v Corporation of Renfrew*[18], a ratepayer objected to the burgh using the common good account or, indeed, any other funds for the purposes of opposing a bill which had been introduced into the House of Commons entitled "An Act to amend the Constitution of the Trustees of the Clyde Navigation, and for other purposes". There were certain defects in the pursuer's pleadings but the main reason for throwing out the action was title to sue. The court held, quoting previous authorities and the institutional writers, that at least in the case of a royal burgh, the only individual with a right to intervene in the corporate actings of a burgh was the Crown, as possessing "a right of oversight and control".

18 (1906) 8 F 905, (1906) 14 SLT 106.

The second case until recently on this point was *D & J Nicol v Dundee Harbour Trustees*[19]. This case concerned the trustees of the harbour of Dundee, a corporation set up by statute to administer Dundee harbour. The harbour trustees had a duty to provide a ferry service but, as a means of obtaining extra income, they used the ferry boats on occasion as excursion steamers. D & J Nicol were in the same line of business and sought an interdict against the harbour trustees from acting in a way which was *ultra vires*.

Lord Dunedin, commenting on the common good cases, said[20]:

> "Now the underlying view of the common good cases was undoubtedly this, that looking to the origin of the common good, and the wide range of discretion given to the Magistrates in its management and application, the Crown, as represented by the Exchequer, could alone institute what one might now call an audit, and that no private burgess could be allowed to do so."

He then went on to point out that this line of cases was only concerned with an audit and that burgesses had been held perfectly capable of having a title and interest to sue in the more common cases dealing with alienation of common good land. In the case before him, he said, the company were ratepayers, electors as far as the trustees were concerned, and persons for whose benefit the harbour was kept up[21].

This question of title and interest was given a modern hearing in *Cockenzie and Port Seton Community Council v East Lothian District Council*[22]. This case, decided in the Outer House before Lord Osborne, concerned the proposed demolition of recreational facilities, including a swimming pool known as the Pond Hall in Port Seton. The subjects were conveyed to the then burgh in 1935 under a title condition that they be used for recreation etc, in connection with the adjacent swimming pool. They passed to the

---

19 1915 SC (HL) 7, 1914 SLT 418.
20 1914 SLT at 422.
21 On audit, see also the three Glasgow Corporation cases on alleged misuse of the common good fund: *Glasgow Corporation v Flint* 1966 SC 108; *Kemp v Glasgow Corporation* 1920 SC (HL) 73, and *Graham v Glasgow Corporation* 1936 SC 108.
22 1997 SLT 81.

district council in 1975 and continued to be used for civic and recreational purposes by members of the local community until 1994, when a new community centre for the area was opened.

On the substantive point regarding alienation of common good property, the court had no difficulty in following the *Magistrates of Kirkcaldy v Marks & Spencer Ltd*[23] case as the recreational facilities had clearly been replaced by new ones, thereby removing the quality of inalienability.

More interesting for the purposes of this section is the discussion by Lord Osborne of the earlier authorities on title and interest to sue. In the first place, he found that any restriction against burgesses raising court proceedings was in the context of royal burghs only, as there the Crown, in the person of the Lord Advocate, in theory would be able to raise such an action on behalf of the burgesses.

Secondly, as he pointed out, the string of case law headed by *Conn v Corporation of Renfrew*[24] related only to cases where the burgesses were attempting to have the accounting of the common good called into question judicially. In general, it had long been accepted that individual burgesses could raise proceedings in respect of any "specific, unlawful or *ultra vires* act". Lord Osborne went on:

> "In addition to these considerations, although this point was not the subject of any submission before me, I feel bound to express doubts as to whether any such restrictive principle as was contended for by the respondents survived the reform of local government effected by the Act of 1973, which, *inter alia*, abolished the former Royal Burghs. It appears to me that there would be strong argument to the effect that the accountability of a District Council holding common good property derived from a former burgh now requires to be considered in relation to the structure of local government as it currently stands. If one were to approach the matter on that basis, it appears to me that no justification could be found for the continuance of the restrictive principle contended for."[25]

There are two conclusions to draw from this judgment. First and

23 1937 SLT 574.
24 (1906) 8 F 905, (1906) 14 SLT 106.
25 1997 SLT at 89.

foremost, it seems to settle beyond any doubt the right of a community council to enter into judicial proceedings on common good matters. There are sound policy reasons behind this. Community councils may have little in the way of resources but they are more likely to be both more representative and organised in expressing their views on common good matters than individual burgesses (if the inhabitants of former burghs can still be called that). Moreover, it would have been somewhat nonsensical given the specific statutory role given by Parliament to community councils if they were not able to take part in proceedings which often deal with matters close to the heart of the local community in former burghs.

The second conclusion to draw from the judgment is that the string of authorities headed by *Conn v Corporation of Renfrew*[26] is now somewhat under threat. Title and interest to sue issues – both for individuals and for community councils – are likely to be limited only to questions of accounting for the common good and in relation to former royal burghs and not other kinds of burgh. Even then, Lord Osborne's judgment seems to cast doubt on whether such a string of authorities can be followed in the context of modern local government structures.

This leads neatly to consideration of the use of common good funds and, in particular, the implications for them of the modern financial regime under which local authorities operate.

3.3   Common good and best value: use of common good funds

Financial scrutiny of local authorities has come a long way since the rudimentary provisions of the Town Councils (Scotland) Act 1900. Councils now operate under a complex system of internal and external audit, statute, subordinate legislation and internal regulation. Management of the common good fund or funds entrusted to each local authority, once again, sits within this overall framework.

26 (1906) 8 F 905, (1906) 14 SLT 106.

The most recent expression of this overall regime can now be found in the Local Government in Scotland Act 2003 and, in particular, Part 1: Best Value and Accountability.

Section 1 puts a duty on all local authorities to make arrangements which secure "best value". Best value is defined (section 1(2)) as "continuous improvement in the performance of the authority's functions". That rather gnomic definition is elucidated slightly by section 1(3), which states that, in securing best value, the local authority shall maintain an appropriate balance among:

"(a) the quality of its performance of its functions;
 (b) the cost to the authority of that performance; and
 (c) the cost to persons of any service provided by it for them on a wholly or partly rechargeable basis."

In maintaining that balance, section 1(4) puts an additional obligation on local authorities to have regard to the four Es of efficiency, effectiveness, economy and equal opportunity. The final factors to weigh up are contribution to the achievement of sustainable development (section 1(5)) and, so far as measurement of improvement of performance, the extent to which the outcomes of that performance have improved.

The policing of this aspect of council finance is carried out by the Controller of Audit and the Accounts Commission for Scotland who originated after local government reorganisation in 1975 by virtue of the Local Government (Scotland) Act 1973[27]. The 1973 Act also remains the foundation for the overall obligation on local authorities to "make arrangements for the proper administration of their financial affairs" (section 95) and the keeping of proper accounts and provision for audit (section 96).

Local government finance operates, therefore, under a strict regime, with the 2003 Act giving extra powers to the Accounts Commission for enforcement in the event of default. But how does this fit with the overall management of the common good fund and the requirement that in administering it, local autho-

---

27 Sections 97–105.

rities have to have regard to the inhabitants of the former burghs[28]?

At the close of each burgh's accounts in 1975, each common good fund was transferred to the appropriate district or islands council. In most cases, the fund has been maintained – subject to any intromissions or additions to it – since then as a separate operative account in that council's (and now, unitary authority's) hands. There are instances where all of the common good funds in the district council's or unitary authority's area were amalgamated into one single common good fund, but this is likely to be unusual[29].

In any event, there would appear to be a theoretical tension between the requirement to maintain best value (ie continuous improvement in the performance of the authority's functions) and regard being had to individual former burghs within the authority's area. Indeed, the maintenance of individual funds of money used only within what are now largely historical boundaries for certain specific purposes, might seem to be intrinsically inimical to the delivery of best value across the authority's whole area.

This paradox may be resolved by treating the maintenance of the common good funds as one of the "functions" of the authority. However, that is not explicit in the legislation relating to the common good and it may be that this tension will surface at some point in the future. Local authorities are not bound to spend the former common good fund only within the boundaries of the former burgh. They are only bound to "have regard" to the interests of the inhabitants of the former burgh. It is therefore technically possible for money to be spent outwith the former burgh if the authority could show that it has had regard to the interests of the former burgh but had chosen to pursue continuous improvement/best value by means of a scheme which did not spend the money wholly within the former burgh area. The provision relating to best value is, of course, from later legislation than that relating to the administration of common good funds and would, therefore, be held to supersede it where there was any conflict.

---

28 The position of the four cities, where regard has to be had to the interests of the whole city area, is considered below.

29 See Appendix V.

No such complication exists in the case of Edinburgh, Glasgow, Dundee and Aberdeen, where the interests of the inhabitants coincide neatly with the authority boundary. It seems unlikely that any of the city authorities could fail to have regard to the interests of the inhabitants in delivering continuous improvement in the performance of the authority's functions.

Finally, on the issue of the use of common good funds, it is worth noting briefly the challenges open to inhabitants of former burghs. As seen above in **3.2**, the *Cockenzie and Port Seton Community Council v East Lothian District Council* case[30] effectively limited the previous case law heavily restricting a ratepayer's right to challenge use of common good funds to the very narrow facts of *Conn v Corporation of Renfrew*[31]. This would seem to suggest that individual burgesses (or, perhaps, community councils), seeking "a general accounting for the management of the common good of a royal burgh"[32] would be prevented from doing so by this case.

However, although Lord Osborne did seem to leave open the possibility that, in relation to an action for judicial review of that nature in relation to a royal burgh, such might be the case, it is suggested that the *Conn* case is now dubious authority, particularly in the case of a community council charged with a statutory obligation of scrutinising a local authority's performance. The more likely defence would be that, given the structure in place of the Accounts Commission, Controller of Audit and various other agencies of central and local government, no such action could be pursued until intervention via the various other agencies had been exhausted as an option[33].

3.4 Maintenance of common good properties

Lastly in this chapter on the administration of the common good,

---

30 1997 SLT 81.

31 (1906) 14 SLT 106, (1906) 8 F 905.

32 1997 SLT at 87.

33 Particularly having regard to the three Glasgow Corporation cases referred to at note 21.

it seems appropriate to comment on the maintenance of common good land and buildings. Whilst there is no specific legal obligation on local authorities to maintain land and buildings held on the common good account to any particular standard or in any other way than the authority maintains its other land and buildings, the peculiarities of the common good fund present some practical difficulties for authorities.

This is because the common good fund – which of course includes all its assets such as land and buildings – is, in asset management terms, a sealed unit. No new common good assets are being created and the only income to the fund apart from interest on monies invested arises from lease rentals, either to external organisations or to other departments of the authority where a notional "rental" is transferred between the individual service budget and the common good fund. Such outright sales of common good property as might take place may produce additional capital receipts.

However, if the common good for each former burgh is treated as an individual, self-financing entity, such common good monies as are left in the fund would, in most cases, be quickly eaten up by the maintenance and repair costs of common good properties. Frequently these are high profile and, in some cases, historic buildings such as former burgh chambers.

A good example would be Dunfermline's magnificent City Chambers, built in the 1870s in the high Victorian, French Gothic style to form a dramatic centrepiece to the town. Whilst it continues to provide that centrepiece to Dunfermline's central streetscape, maintenance of such magnificence does not come cheaply and that is replicated amongst many common good properties throughout the country.

The answer most authorities reach as regards this difficulty is for services occupying common good properties to pick up the maintenance bill directly. Such improvements and repairs paid for by other services are likely to be treated as a contribution to the common good fund[34]. Similarly, where external bodies have occu-

---

34 See *Kirkcaldy District Council v Burntisland Community Council* 1993 SLT 753, discussed at **8.3**.

pation of a common good property by way of lease, the FRI (Full Repairing and Insuring) model is usually used.

However, the practice across the country does not appear to be uniform and is not even uniform within authorities. Some properties are maintained at the expense of the common good fund whilst others are paid for by other departments[35]. In addition, this relationship between the common good property and other departments works only in so far as the common good property is capable of beneficial occupation. Unfortunately, some such properties are not capable of such occupation and face the prospect of deterioration and disrepair unless authorities are willing to either dispose of them if another beneficial use can be found, or maintain an empty and surplus to requirements property. The third option is, of course, demolition.

Demolition, and the doctrine that a local authority cannot "plead its own neglect" as a justification for seeking demolition of a common good property, are dealt with more fully in **6.3** and **8.1**. In the meantime, it is worth noting in passing the opinion of Lord Penrose in the case of *Stirling District Council, Petitioners*[36]. That case concerned a building known as the Museum Hall in Bridge of Allan. In his judgment, Lord Penrose said:

> "I am satisfied that it would be unreasonable to refuse the prayer of the petition on the ground that [the building's] state was the responsibility of the petitioners, and to leave the petitioners exposed to the obligations relating to the structure which would follow from their ownership of a listed building which had to be restored for public use."

In that case, the fault for the building's state of repair was not wholly that of the district council and its predecessors as there were also soil conditions which had caused settlement and structural damage. As will be seen, it may be that local authorities are not under a direct obligation to maintain common good properties. However, there may well be an argument that if they allow them

---

35 See Appendix V.
36 Outer House, 19 May 2000, unreported: available on www.scotcourts. gov.uk.

to fall into disrepair – and that disrepair is wholly their fault – then they might be compelled to do something about it by the court.

Consideration of this topic leads on to common good property generally. Before the vexed question of when it can and cannot be disposed of is considered, it is prudent to look at how common good property and its attendant speciality of title might be classified and, ultimately, identified.

Chapter 4

Inalienable common good land

4.1 Moveable common good property and other rarities

Most common good cases, and most common good property left today, consist of heritable property of the usual kind: land and buildings. However, it should be recognised that all sorts of things have in the past fallen into the common good, often as a result of the original burgh charter. Oddities such as the right of patronage of a second ministerial charge in the church[1]; the right to hold markets (which, as will be seen, was effectively also an obligation)[2]; and petty customs[3] may no longer trouble anyone today. Harbour dues are often a feature of burgh charters, but it is not entirely clear whether they have survived the 1975 reorganisation of local government which gave the statutory responsibility for harbours to regional councils[4].

Other types of rights which may still be relevant, dependent on environmental factors, are *regalia minora* such as salmon fishings[5] and the right to collect mussel scalps or other products of the sea-

---

1 *Trades of St Andrews v Magistrates and Town Council of St Andrews* 27 Feb 1824 FC.

2 *Blackie v Magistrates of Edinburgh* (1884) 11 R 783; and see **4.4**.

3 *Magistrates of Lochmaben v Beck* (1841) 4 D 16; *Kerr v Magistrates of Linlithgow* (1865) 3 M 370.

4 See **2.2**. Harbours, incidentally, are likely to form part of the inalienable part of the common good, at least so far as partial disposal is concerned: see *Anstruther v Pollock, Gilmour & Co* (1868) 6 SLR 161.

5 *Fram v Magistrates of Dumbarton* (1786) Mor 2002.

shore[6]. It will also be interesting to see whether the case of *Threshie v Magistrates and Town Council of Annan*, where the High Street of Annan was held to be the responsibility of the burgh for maintenance, and not that of the statutory road trustees for the road between Dumfries and Carlisle of which it formed part, still has relevance in some maintenance dispute in the future[7].

One type of property which has not featured strongly in a significant amount of case law is moveable property. However, it is quite likely that the larger burghs in particular will have substantial amounts of moveable property – ceremonial robes, antique furniture and even works of art, which may be of substantial value. One could well imagine, for example, that the sale of works of art – or even their long-term loan to galleries outwith the burgh – might raise emotive issues in the present day.

Unfortunately, there seems to be only one case which could be said to deal with moveable property as such. In *Magistrates of Dumbarton v University of Edinburgh*[8], the original Dumbarton burgh charter had turned up in the estate of a dead antiquarian who had bequeathed it with the rest of his interesting manuscripts to the University of Edinburgh. It had vanished from Dumbarton during Court of Session litigation in 1813, never to return. The court held that the charter was inalienable property forming part of the common good. It would seem that the court took a similar view to other types of common good cases.

It is time to turn now to heritable property and, in particular, to land and buildings, bearing in mind that the principles established as regards the classifications of common good property, and

---

6 *Magistrates of St Andrews v Wilson* (1869) 7 M 1105. It is interesting to note that, in both of these cases, the court came to a conclusion that allowed a form of alienation as long as the burgesses obtained preferential rates for the salmon and mussel scalps.

7 *Threshie v Magistrates and Town Council of Annan* (1845) 8 D 276 at 281 per Lord Mackenzie: "a road is only for travelling, while a street is for markets and meetings – for a paved way between the houses – for conveying water and gas to the houses – and subject to the jurisdiction of the magistrates, as much as the houses are".

8 (1909) 1 SLT 51.

the prohibition at common law on alienation, would seem to apply
with equal force to all types of property.

4.2 *Murray* and the three categories

In the present day, when dealing with heritable property formerly
held by a burgh, the most common question asked is: "Is it
common good?" Actually, that question often means one, or both,
of two things:

> ➤ does the property form part of the common good of the
> burgh, or
> ➤ is it subject to some kind of prohibition, or restriction, on
> alienation *as a result of being part of the common good*?

These two questions form the central topic for the next two
chapters. The question of whether property forms part of the
common good, or indeed whether all burgh property is common
good, is reserved for chapter 5. The question of whether a sub-
group of common good property is subject to special rules on
alienation is dealt with in this chapter.

If it seems odd to deal with the classification of a sub-group
ahead of classification of the group itself, there is at least a sound
reason based on chronology. The nineteenth-century case law concerned itself principally with determining which burgh property
had a "quality of inalienability" to it, with the issue of whether or
not *all* burgh property was held on the common good being
addressed by twentieth-century case law.

Sitting in the Outer House of the Court of Session on 12
November 1892, the Lord Ordinary, Lord Kincairney, produced
this definition of the restrictive nature of common good title
within burghs:

> "I think it is now completely settled that questions of this nature
> as to the limits of the powers to the magistrates of burghs in deal-
> ing with burgh property are not questions in the law of servitude,
> or in the law of prescription, but questions as to the quality of title
> of the magistrates. Further, it is clear that the magistrates have full
> power to alienate the heritable property of a burgh, unless a con-

dition or quality limiting their powers be impressed on their title either by its express terms or by usage interpreting their title."[9]

This is to be contrasted with the earlier nineteenth-century approach to categorise the types of public use of land then most relevant, such as bleaching or organised recreation of some sort, as a sort of servitude. This approach was abandoned for land owned by burghs themselves in the case of *Home v Young*[10], a case mentioned earlier at **1.2**.

It is conceivable, however, that local authorities could still vindicate the rights of burgh inhabitants in questions with neighbouring proprietors in "time immemorial" cases of possession using a servitude argument. Most of the nineteenth-century cases are unhelpful to such a claim. It has been held that there are no servitudes of fishing[11]; curling[12]; promenading[13]; and pasturage[14]. A rare success for the residents in this string of case law is in relation to taking water from wells and bleaching clothes on land owned by a neighbouring proprietor, who was also, significantly, the feudal superior of the burgh of barony[15].

Another case vindicating the rights of burgh residents over non-burgh property – this time in relation to golf – is *Magistrates of Earlsferry v Malcolm*[16]. However, the case could be viewed as reflecting the judges' suspicion that the neighbouring landowner had encroached on the land of a burgh with few resources to resist.

Other tools of property law were used in the mid-nineteenth century to describe the relationship between the magistrates, the inhabitants and the property. One such tool was to describe the

---

  9 *Murray v Magistrates of Forfar* (1893) 1 SLT 105, (1893) 20 R 908 at 914.
10 (1846) 9 D 286.
11 *Fergusson v Shirreff* (1844) 6 D 1363.
12 *Harvey v Lindsay* (1853) 15 D 768.
13 *Dyce v Hay* (1849) 11 D 1266, affd (1852) 1 Macq 305.
14 *Feuars of Dunse v Hay* (1732) Mor 1824.
15 *Sinclair v Magistrates of Dysart* (1779) Mor 14519; affd sub nom *St Clair v Magistrates of Dysart* (1780) 2 Pat 554. But cf *Town of Falkland v Carmichael* (1708) Mor 10916; *Duke of Roxburghe v Jeffray* (1755) Mor 2340, revsd (1757) 1 Pat 632.
16 (1829) 7 S 755, (1832) 11 S 74.

relationship as analogous to that of trustees; a doctrine now discarded in favour of the "quality of title" approach[17].

Another way of looking at the issue of inalienable common good property is to describe the land itself as being a different type of property from other property. It is said to be *res universitatis*, or *extra commercium*, a thing held in the form of public ownership that renders it incapable of being alienated[18].

Turning back to Lord Kincairney's dicta, it can be seen that some "burgh property" is affected by a "quality of title" to the extent that it cannot be alienated. Some "burgh property", it would seem, is not so affected. But which is which?

The case from which Lord Kincairney's Outer House dicta are taken seems to provide part at least of the answer. This is *Murray v Magistrates of Forfar*[19], a case representing the high watermark of nineteenth-century reasoning on common good and inalienability.

The case concerned a large area of ground then situated at the edge of Forfar known as the Market Muir. From time immemorial (a phrase considered in more detail later on), the land had been used in terms of the burgh charter on eight particular days in the year for public horse and cattle markets. For the rest of the year, the evidence established, the same area of land had been used for walking and exercise and games such as golf, shinty, cricket, football and quoiting and for "other exercises and recreations and for bleaching clothes".

However, the days of eight markets a year were numbered. The traditional operations were facing stiff competition from the recent introduction into the town of an auction mart which held weekly horse and cattle markets. The magistrates proposed to lease the ground for a similar purpose, to the exclusion of the recreational uses that the residents had previously enjoyed over the ground. A local doctor sought an interdict against the magistrates to prevent them from doing this.

---

17 The cases cited in **1.4** seem to have closed the door on that interpretation for good.

18 See R R M Paisley, *Land Law* (2000), para 1.26.

19 (1893) 20 R 908, (1893) 1 SLT 105.

In determining that interdict should be granted and the proposed lease prevented, Lord McLaren came to the following view of "public rights" in what he variously called "common land" and "burgh property":

> "It appears to me that in the most extended view which can be taken of the constitution of public rights of this description, there are at least three ways in which a public use of burgh property may be acquired. The land may be appropriated to public uses in the Charter or original grant; the land, after it is vested in a public body, such as a Town-Council, may be irrevocably appropriated to public uses by the act of the Town-Council itself; and, again, it may be so appropriated, or rather the inference may be drawn that it was originally appropriated to public uses from evidence that the land has been so used and enjoyed for time immemorial."[20]

This often quoted dictum was the fullest exposition of what might constitute inalienable common good land so far. Indeed, it built upon the dicta of Lord Kincairney quoted at the start of this chapter. Instead of two categories of common good land, either that which had a condition expressing it as such in its title or a construction being placed upon the quality of the magistrates' title by "usage", Lord McLaren had produced "at least" three categories.

Apart from a specific dedication in the title, there was now dedication by the actings of the magistrates themselves, or by the fact that a public use had grown up from time immemorial which the magistrates had not tried to stop. It is not clear what other categories his Lordship might have had in mind by his use of the phrase "at least", and these three categories appear to be the only ones recognised now. Each of them falls to be examined now in turn, by reference to the case law.

However, it is important to recognise at the outset exactly what is being classified. Under the *Murray* doctrine, it is possible to classify types of common good land which have a quality of inalienability to them and which, according to the 1973 Act's wording, might therefore attract a "question" as to the right of the authority to alienate them. This does not comprise all common good land.

---

20 At 918–919.

As will be seen in the next chapter, that is a separate task and one which is very far from straightforward.

4.3   Use from time immemorial by the public

Having just looked at the *Murray* case, and its three classifications, it seems appropriate to start with the classification of land which applied in the case itself. Their Lordships had listened to witnesses on the previous uses of the Market Muir, including the Provost of Forfar who, in his seventy-second year, was able to remember quoits, ninepins and, more recently, cricket and football, having been played "without objection or hindrance". His recollection of what had happened when he was a young man clearly took the concept of "time immemorial" beyond the bounds of the then long negative prescription period of forty years, and, presumably, beyond the memories of most of the people in the court beyond the Provost and, perhaps, their Lordships themselves.

The case is also interesting for its treatment of that part of the Market Muir which did not date back to the original charter of 1665 but had been acquired as an addition to it in 1853. So far as this piece of land was concerned, the court found that there was evidence that the property had been acquired as an investment with a view to resale for housing development. In addition, Lord McLaren said:

> "Again, it cannot well be maintained that the inhabitants or bur-
> gesses have acquired a right to restrain the council from alienating
> this property by immemorial use, and for this conclusive reason,
> that the title of the burgh was obtained within the prescriptive per-
> iod, and such use as the public has enjoyed falls short of the period
> of forty years which in our law is taken to be equivalent to im-
> memorial possession in questions of public rights or use explana-
> tory of such rights."[21]

However, Lord McLaren went slightly further than that at the end of his judgment by seeming to suggest that as well as public

---

21 At 919.

use for a period exceeding the then prescriptive period, the title had
to be what he described as "ancient". He said:

> "It is not necessary to consider what would be the effect of a use
> of un-enclosed land by the public existing for a period exceeding
> forty years. Supposing the Town-Council to assert the rights as
> proprietors on all suitable occasions, I hesitate to say that the pro-
> prietor shall be held to lose his rights, or to have assented to a
> qualification of his rights, by the mere fact that members of the
> public had walked or sported on the lands, and that the proprietor
> has not treated their access as trespass. But as this question may arise
> hereafter, I do not wish to give an opinion upon it."[22]

It seems, therefore, for the public to have acquired public rights
over the ground which would prevent its alienation, the use must,
as far as possible, be at the limits of living memory and the title
to the land should be "ancient". As will be seen, the situation is
different where the authority has in effect dedicated the land in
question to that use.

One of the cases referred to as sound authority for this classification of common good land was the 1859 case of *Sanderson v Lees*[23].
In this case, one Henry Sanderson, designed "surgeon, an inhabi-
tant of Musselburgh and also a burgess thereof, and member of the
Musselburgh Golf Club" brought an action of interdict against the
local authority and the builder who had been intending to develop
part of Musselburgh links. The case report does not set out the facts
in any great detail but, according to Lord Deas[24], the plan was to
lay out several streets on the links.

As in other cases, there had been previous alienations of land at
the edges of the links for building. However, Mr Sanderson, concerned that the current development would seriously interrupt his
golf game, took action. A previous case[25] had already established

---

22 At 920.
23 (1859) 22 D 24.
24 At 32.
25 *Cathie v Magistrates of Musselburgh* (1752) Mor 2521. The very brief case
    report states: "Magistrates of a Burgh of Regality have the same power
    with Magistrates of a Royal Burgh, to grant feus of the common good of
    the burgh. This was the unanimous opinion of the court."

the immemorial use of the links of Musselburgh for recreation and particularly the playing of golf.

The court found in favour of Mr Sanderson. It held that the right to exercise and play golf over the links was not in the nature of servitude but a quality of the title. Lord Curriehill said:

> "It has been held, that although the property is vested in the Corporation . . . yet one of the purposes for which it is so vested in them is to hold it for the use of the inhabitants or others, to the effect of their enjoying the privileges which they have so exercised; that this would be an unquestionably good title in law if that purpose had been distinctly expressed in the Charters of Incorporation of the burgh; and that although it be not so particularly set forth in those Charters, yet the immemorial usage following upon them are sufficient to explain the general terms in which they are expressed, so as to show that such was their meaning and effect."[26]

Nor was the court impressed with the suggestion that the proposed disposal would leave enough room for golf to be played, although there seemed to be some suggestion that, if the magistrates wished to bring an action of declarator that the immemorial use could be limited in some way to a specified portion, that might be entertained[27].

These two issues of previous encroachment and whether the proposed encroachment would interfere with the public use were further explored in another golfing case, *Paterson v Magistrates of St Andrews*[28].

In this case, the magistrates of St Andrews had feued off pieces of land at the edges of the famous golf course in the past. In particular, they had feued off a strip along the southern boundary where it abutted the main road, and, on this strip, houses had been built from around 1820. Access was being taken to the houses via a road at the edge of the links and this was now being cut up by traffic. However, when the magistrates resolved to build a 21-foot-wide metalled road for the general use of the public as well as of the

---

26 (1859) 22 D at 30.

27 See, in particular, Lord Pitmilly's judgment at the foot of 27, and that of Lord Deas at the foot of 32.

28 (1880) 7 R 712, (1881) 8 R (HL) 117.

occupiers of the houses, this was objected to as an encroachment
on the rights of the inhabitants and, in particular, their golfing
rights. The land did not form part of the regular part of the links
but could be easily reached with a misdirected shot.

The Second Division of the Inner House held that the magistrates were allowed to build the road but not to dispose of the *solum*
of the road, or to alienate the administration and control of it.

On the question of previous alienations, the Lord Justice-Clerk,
Lord Moncrieff, made it clear that he considered the previous feus
had been "originally a violation of the rights of the community"
but that they had been placed "beyond challenge" by prescription.
There was no question, however, that previous alienations could
justify any further ones. However, so far as a road was concerned,
the Lord Justice-Clerk said:

> "I have come to the opinion that this is an act of fair and reasonable
> administration, and so within the discretion of the Magistrates. I
> think they may allow the surface of this strip of ground to be so
> metalled as is proposed and so used as long as they think that
> operation and use conducive to the benefit of the community, and
> consistent with the ordinary purposes of recreation to which the
> ground has hitherto been put. There is no obligation incumbent
> on the civic authority to keep every square yard of these commons
> in grass. They may make footpaths through them, or flower-beds,
> or clumps of plantation, where these do not interfere with the
> more primary destination. They might maintain a lawn-tennis
> ground or a skating rink, or an alcove for a band of music, and
> they might gravel, or causeway, or pave the accesses leading to
> these places . . . all these things are pure acts of ordinary and rea-
> sonable administration, which not only do not infer any alienation
> of the *solum*, but do not affect any permanent alteration on the sur-
> face, as these uses are in their nature temporary."[29]

Their Lordships were clearly much taken with the evidence of
"ten of the best known amateur players" who gave the opinion
that the introduction of a road would improve the golf course as a
golfing links if anything (presumably by giving a better lie for all
those misdirected shots). The case was appealed to the House of

29 (1880) 7 R at 725–726.

Lords but it adhered to the Inner House decision, subject only to the slight amendment that the town council was put under the obligation of ensuring that no-one else would acquire title to or interfere with the administration of the road.

These three nineteenth-century cases, then, show a use being created by the public with the magistrates effectively acquiescing to that use. It could be argued that there is a very fine line between the public taking matters into their own hands and the magistrates intending to make areas of land in particular dedicated to those uses – the second category considered below.

One limitation to this present category, however, is that the use by the public must be meaningful and consistent. Lord Kincairney in the *Murray*[30] case referred to the evidence on the playing of games over the Muir as being "monotonous, uniform, consistent and frequently repeated". In contrast, there have been cases where the evidence of recreation was not sufficient to qualify the title of the magistrates. The principal authority here is *Montgomerie and Company Ltd v Wallace-James*[31].

That case concerned an acre of ground on the west bank of the River Tyne in Haddington and whether it had been used in time immemorial for the use and enjoyment of the burgesses and the inhabitants of the burgh. With some hesitation, the House of Lords reversed concurrent judgments of the Lord Ordinary and the Inner House of the Court of Session, as they considered that the evidence which had been advanced in the lower courts was not sufficient to show immemorial possession by the public. Their Lordships were particularly influenced by the configuration of the ground – described as a narrow strip along the side of a river varying in width at different times[32], the fact that it had been leased for the making of lime between 1857 and 1866 to private individuals, thus interrupting the public's possession[33], and the lack of evidence of public use generally.

In this connection, Lord Shand said:

30 (1893) 20 R at 912.
31 (1903) 6 F (HL) 10, (1903) 11 SLT 537.
32 At 538 per the Lord Chancellor.
33 At 539 per Lord Shand.

"With the removal of [the lime stances] there was some further use of the same kind for playing and for walking exercise, but nothing occurred of such a use as systematic golf and cricket, or games of that class, and no such constant and persistent uses as to indicate appropriations where that has been held to have taken place in previous cases.

"In regard to the drying and bleaching of clothes, even at the time after the stances were removed, the use of the ground seems to have been made to much the greater extent after the erection of the wash-houses by the persons who paid and used for that accommodation. Any use beyond that was trifling in kind and was not, I think, taken or thought of as a matter of right, or as given or allowed by the Burgh as an appropriation to the public."[34]

In summary then, the classification of common good land which has become inalienable by public use is one that very much turns upon the facts of each case. Previous alienations of parts of the same property do not prejudice the rights of the burgesses to object to further proposed alienations. At the same time, alienations which are not inconsistent with the public use are likely to be allowed. The public use must be consistent, be at least for the long, negative, prescriptive period, and not be interrupted by private use of the land to any great extent. It is certainly preferable if the title is suitably ancient.

One issue which is not dealt with here but which does arise with this classification of common good property is alienation arising from the neglect of the magistrates – ie properties becoming derelict and the magistrates then claiming that the public use has ceased. This topic will be dealt with at **8.1**.

4.4 Dedication for public uses

As explained above, it is sometimes a fine line between a local authority having consciously dedicated a building or piece of land to some form of public use and – at least in the case of land – that public use having appeared organically of its own volition. However, there is a clear string of cases which indicates that property which has been specifically dedicated to "public" uses may, at the very least, have alienation issues, as it were.

Although most recent cases concern public buildings which were former burgh chambers, the classification is much wider than that. Lord Jamieson, in the *Magistrates of Kirkcaldy v Marks & Spencer Ltd* case[35] referred to Erskine's Institutes (II.i.7), in referring to "town houses, market places, churchyards, public streets and corporation halls".

It would be misleading to assume that burghs historically were all-powerful and owned everything necessary for the administration of a burgh. At various points other sets of trustees such as the harbour trustees in the *D & J Nicol* case[36] or police commissioners performed some of the public functions required for a burgh. It is interesting to note, for example, the case of *Thom, Petitioner*[37] where the clerk to the Linlithgow Police Commissioners successfully petitioned the court for authority to sell a portion of the flesh market (ie where meat was sold) which had been acquired in terms of the General Police and Improvement Act 1862 but which was surplus to requirements. He required to do that because there was no specific power to dispose of the property in the statutory framework the trustees operated under.

However, it is fair to say that throughout the ebb and flow of local government administration over the last two centuries, burghs have, in general, held many types of property which could be said to have been "dedicated to public use" in that they were necessary to the economic and social viability of the burgh.

One early example can be found in the case of *Phin v Magistrates of Auchtermuchty*[38]. Like many burghs in the 1820s and 1830s, the burgh of Auchtermuchty had got into financial difficulties and an action of adjudication had been raised by a creditor for the whole property of the burgh. Decree of adjudication was pronounced and following upon this the creditor sought to sell off the property.

---

35 1937 SLT 574 at 576.
36 1915 SC (HL) 7, 1914 SLT 418; see **3.2**.
37 (1887) 14 R 444.
38 (1827) 5 S 690.

Included amongst this was the town house and jail with a large bell in the steeple of the town house which could not have been removed without taking down part of the steeple, as well as the petty customs of the burgh, a form of local taxation which the magistrates could impose at the market under the terms of their royal charter.

The burgh and the Officers of State on behalf of the Crown objected to the sale of these items as they claimed they were *res universitatis* and incapable of being alienated.

The court, with one dissension, agreed. Lord Pitmilly said:

> "The burgh could not sell these subjects voluntarily, except in the case of their having provided new ones for the use of the burgh, when they might dispose of the old buildings no longer used as a jail, &c, and if the burgh could not sell, it necessarily follows that the creditors cannot attach them. The salary of public officers cannot be attached to the extent of preventing them from performing the duty for which the salary is given; and in like manner, the buildings, &c of a burgh destined for public purposes, cannot be attached so as to defeat the purposes for which they had been established."[39]

Lord Alloway dissented to the extent that he thought the jail, which was derelict, was of no further public use given that the burgh was not in a state to enable it to repair the jail[40].

Another case concerning property – or perhaps more properly a right – of this classification is *Blackie v Magistrates of Edinburgh*[41]. This case concerned the fruit and vegetable market held on what is now the site of the Waverley Shopping Centre, and the length of the report may have something to do with the personal interest of their Lordships in such an Edinburgh institution as the market.

The magistrates had, by Royal Charters culminating in the so-called "Golden Charter" of James VI of 1603, been given a right to hold markets within the burgh. Throughout the nineteenth century, the site of the market had moved from time to time as con-

---

39 (1827) 5 S at 692.
40 On petty customs, see also *Kerr v Magistrates of Linlithgow* (1865) 3 M 370; and **4.1**.
41 (1884) 11 R 783.

struction of the railway went on about it. Then the magistrates closed the market to the market gardeners for a period of three weeks to hold a fisheries exhibition, banishing the market gardeners to the streets around the market hall for that period.

The court held that excluding the market gardeners for a period of three weeks from the market hall, even where unenclosed space was made available to them in the surrounding streets, was unlawful. Although the case was partly determined on the basis of local byelaws and statutes and the specific obligations under them of the magistrates, Lord Shand in particular commented on the common law position:

> "And as I cannot doubt that, under the statutes, the market-place is vested in the corporation primarily for the purpose of affording proper and suitable accommodation for the purchase and sale of fruit and vegetables, the corporation is bound *ante omnia* to give effect to that purpose. Such an appropriation and use of the market [ie three weeks for a fisheries exhibition] as the pursuers complain of, seems to me to amount to a disregard of the primary purpose for which the market is held, and of the consequent obligations of the defenders, and cannot be defended on the ground that it is within the bounds of a due and ordinary exercise of discretion."[42]

It would be interesting to see whether this precedent is ever used in the context of the revival in farmers' markets which take place in many former burghs nowadays.

This leads on to the leading case in this classification, that of *Magistrates of Kirkcaldy v Marks & Spencer Ltd*[43]. This case was examined earlier, in the context of its influence on the Local Government (Scotland) Act 1947, at **2.1**. The former burgh chambers were to be sold to Marks & Spencer; a new town house was to be built; and, in the meantime, the meetings of the council were to take place in the burgh court which formed part of the police administration buildings. The court held that this arrangement would not lead to inefficient administration of public business or detract from the "dignity of the burgh". Accordingly, the alienation was lawful.

42 (1884) 11 R at 802.
43 1937 SLT 574.

4.5   Common good nature arising from grant

At **1.4**, some time was spent looking at common good properties arising from a grant in distinguishing them from properties which had been given over to burghs in the form of a public trust. It was seen that, despite the liberal use of the word "trust" at various points in a conveyance, in most cases properties which had been gifted to the burgh for some specific public purpose – for use as a park, perhaps, or for some form of public building such as a museum or theatre – would form part of the common good rather than constituting a public trust.

In **2.4** properties of this type were looked at again in the context of feudal reform and it was seen that the quality of title which gave rise to their inalienability seemed likely to have survived the impact of feudal reform even if the relevant title conditions could no longer be enforced by the superior himself.

With this in view, there is not much more that needs to be said about properties in this third classification. By their nature, it will be obvious that these properties form part of the common good generally to a far greater extent than the other two classifications already discussed. The matter is literally there in black and white in the title deed. The intention of the disponers is clear – or usually is.

It is no coincidence that properties of this classification tend to come from the mid to late nineteenth century and thereafter. Following the Industrial Revolution and the widespread disposal of the community's patrimony, benefactors wished to ensure that their intentions could not be misinterpreted. Examples of typical wordings would be:

"I do hereby give, grant and dispone to and in favour of the Provost, Magistrates and Town Council of the Burgh of Hamilton and as such representing the community of the said burgh and their successors in office for behoof of the whole body and community of the said burgh .... It shall not be lawful to nor in the power of my said disponees or their foresaids to sell, alienate, or dispone the said subjects hereby conveyed or any part thereof but the same shall be held in trust always for behoof of and solely for the use, recreation and enjoyment of the inhabitants of the Burgh of Hamilton and shall be used as a public park or recreational ground only ...."[44]

"[The property] shall be used as a public hall, council chambers, offices and public refreshment and recreation rooms and offices in connection therewith and in connection with the [adjacent] swimming pond ...... provided always that the said buildings shall always be appropriated to and for uses and purposes for which the same shall originally be erected or for uses and purposes similar thereto and not inconsistent therewith."[45]

"As a gift to be used for the general purposes of the town."[46]

It need hardly be said that each case, and each title, will turn upon the specific wording and the expressed intentions of the disponer if these can be clearly shown outwith the bounds of the deed itself.

Having looked at the three classifications of what is generally known as common good property following the *Murray* case, it is time now to look at a case which answers a more fundamental question, namely what is and is not part of the common good so far as property is concerned: the *Ruthin Castle* case.

---

44 *South Lanarkshire Council, Petitioners* Inner House, 11 August 2004, unreported.
45 *Cockenzie and Port Seton Community Council v East Lothian District Council* 1997 SLT 81.
46 *Fife Council v Leven Community Council* Kirkcaldy Sh Ct, 25 July 2001, unreported.

Chapter 5

Classification of common good land

5.1 When is burgh property part of the common good?

Chapter 4 outlined how some common good property could be classified as being a type of property to which a quality of inalienability, exercisable by the residents of the burgh, applied. It is clear from the case law that such a quality does not apply to all common good property formerly held by burghs. More fundamentally, however, how can it be established in the first place whether former burgh property falls into the common good?

To say the answer to this is not straightforward is something of an understatement. There is no magic formula for identifying the common good property in a burgh. The simplistic approach of checking the former burgh's common good accounts to establish whether any particular property was identified in the accounts as being held as part of the common good has been judicially disapproved of in the case of *Cockenzie and Port Seton Community Council v East Lothian District Council*, encountered earlier[1]. In that case Lord Osborne said:

> "Furthermore, it appears to me that the features of the accounts of the burgh which were relied upon by the respondents do not carry them very far. The way in which property is treated in accounts may or may not correctly reflect the classification of that property according to appropriate legal criteria."[2]

In that case, a minute of a finance sub-committee of the burgh

1 1997 SLT 81; see **3.2** and **3.3**.
2 At 89.

council from around the time of the building of the subjects was produced. This showed that the council had decided that it should consider transferring some of the profits of the swimming pool and buildings connected with it to set up a common good fund for the burgh. It was clear, therefore, as Lord Osborne pointed out[3], that the council did not consider the swimming pool and buildings to be common good property. Similarly, the accounts of the burgh of Cockenzie and Port Seton in 1957 made no reference to the swimming pool being part of the common good and, again, in 1975, when the swimming pool and buildings appeared reflected in the general income and expenditure account of the burgh. Despite all of that the property was held to form part of the common good.

It is clear from the recent case law, then, that how a property asset has been treated in the common good account is virtually no guide at all as to whether it does form part of the common good – although it is submitted that the existence of a building in the common good account might be more likely to be treated as persuasive evidence than the other way round.

The answer to the question of whether burgh property is common good or not can largely be drawn from a single case, albeit one that is out of the ordinary in almost every way.

5.2   The *Ruthin Castle* case

The case of *Magistrates of Banff v Ruthin*[4] *Castle Ltd*[5] does not, at least at first, blend in easily with the rest of the case law on common good land. It relies on a peculiar set of facts. The judgments seem to ignore vast amounts of previous case law – and, in particular, the *Murray* classifications looked at in chapter 4. And although the case is fundamentally about whether or not a property fell into the

---

3 At 85.
4 Although, given the north-east location of the case, Ruthin might seem to be a misprint for Ruthvin or Ruthven, this is not, in fact, the case. Ruthin is the name of the company's Welsh base.
5 1944 SLT 373.

common good of the burghs involved, their Lordships only really get themselves exercised in relation to a conveyancing point arguably even more arcane than the nature of common good title.

The facts were touched on at **1.4** but it is worth setting them out in a little more detail now because they bear a heavy influence on the way the case was decided. The case was brought by the burghs of Banff and MacDuff, as joint proprietors of an estate known as Duff House. It was brought as an action of declarator and payment against Ruthin Castle Ltd as tenants under the major part of a lease of the property, for declarator that the lease was valid and for payment of the last term's rent.

In 1906, Banff in particular seems to have been keen to turn itself into the type of seaside resort so beloved of the Edwardians, but lacked land for a golf course and other recreational facilities which would draw in holidaymakers. The Duke of Fife was a local magnate and heard of this. He offered to grant, as a free gift, the mansion of Duff House and a large portion of its grounds to the burghs of Banff and MacDuff. In a letter offering the gift, he said that he was convinced that the "corporations of the two towns will know how to act for their material advantage as well as for the recreation and well-being of the community". The letter went on to say that "the scheme would have an additional value in that it would bring together Banff and MacDuff which are such close neighbours and whose interests should always be identical". For this reason, he proposed to grant the disposition in favour of both burghs jointly.

There is some evidence that there was an attempt to avoid the property falling into the common good of both burghs from the very start. The town clerk of Banff apparently tried to have additional wording put in the disposition to set the gift up as a separate trust. However, the Duke of Fife was having none of this and insisted on the deeds showing an unconditional gift. However, at some point in the drafting of the disposition, the unusual formula was arrived at of a disposition to the provost, magistrates and councillors of both burghs and "to their joint assignees, heritably and irredeemably". This "joint destination" was a point which most exercised their Lordships in the Inner House judgment. The concept of a joint destination which had the effect of neither party having a *pro indiviso* right was a concept alien to Scots law and their Lordships were anxious to make sure it stayed a stranger. However, fortunately, it is not necessary to look into that point here.

The disposition was duly granted and recorded. This was the era of section 98 of the Town Councils (Scotland) Act 1900, covered in **2.1**. That provision required "all feus, alienations or tacks for more than five years of any heritable property of the burgh, or vested in the council, so far as forming part of the common good" to proceed by public roup. For whatever reason, the joint burghs did not want to dispose of the property by public roup. They came to a private bargain in 1909 with a company known as Duff House Limited. The lease was from 15 May 1909 for ninety-nine years. There seems little doubt that this lease was not a particularly good deal for the landlords. The rent was either not capable of review or, at the very least, had not been reviewed for some thirty-two years by the time the case came to court in 1941. Lord Mackay, in his judgment, commented acidly:

> "I pause here for a moment simply to express a vivid doubt as to whether upon any sort of right held by councils over their burgh properties this transaction could have been justified as one truly for the benefit of the community."[6]

Whatever the rights and wrongs of the transaction, the lease proceeded. It was assigned in 1913 to another company called the New Duff House Sanitarium Limited[7] in an attempt to use the property as a sanatorium. This appears to have been unsuccessful, since at the end of 1922 the company acquired other subjects at Ruthin in Wales, to which it removed its staff and equipment, leaving only a caretaker at Duff House. In 1931 the company altered its name to Ruthin Castle Limited. There was a sub-lease for use of the property as a hotel, but that use also seems to have failed and in October 1939 the subjects were requisitioned by the War Office as an internment camp. Presumably some kind of compensation will have been paid for this but it appears to have been paid to the tenants.

---

6 At 378.
7 Again, "Sanitarium" appears to be the actual spelling of the company as it is repeated several times in the judgment.

The property was clearly something of a white elephant and, in 1940, the tenants hit upon the idea that they might find a way out of a lease which had obviously become a loss-making burden on them. Accordingly, they wrote to the burghs claiming that the lease was void *ab initio*. The property fell into the common good of both burghs, they argued, and, as such, should have been advertised by public roup in terms of the Town Councils (Scotland) Act 1900. The fact that a deal had been done by private bargain with their predecessors invalidated the lease.

This, then, was the quite narrow question before the court. If the property could be said to form part of the common good of the two burghs, then the lease was at an end. If it was not, and it was held instead under some form of special trust, as the burghs argued, then the lease would still be in existence and the rent would be payable. The effect of this would be that a lease which their Lordships clearly thought was a bad bargain for the people of the burghs would remain in existence until May 2008 unless brought to an end by other means. It was hardly a conclusion that Court of Session judges, with an eye to the general good of the public, could stomach.

It is perhaps surprising then that the joint burghs were successful at the first instance in the Outer House. Lord Stevenson, without allowing a proof before answer, held that the property did not form part of the common good. He said:

> "If additions [to the common good] are made, they must necessarily be held on the same conditions as the original grant [ie the Charter of the Burgh]. They must be at the uncontrolled discretion of the Magistrates, to be used as they think fit for the benefit of the burgh. The gift of the Duke of Fife does not comply with this condition. The title is in the name of the two burghs as joint owners. Every act of administration must be done by or on behalf of both burghs. The Magistrates of one burgh cannot let the subject of the gift, nor exercise any act of dominium over it, nor can the property or any part thereof be set aside for the exclusive use of either burgh."

This judgment was not particularly well reasoned given that many additions to the common good over the previous century had been given specifically into the common good but under conditions – the types of grant by benefactors examined in some detail already in **1.4** and **4.5**. The defenders reclaimed and, as a first step, the Inner House ordered a proof before answer to investigate the peculiar facts of the case in a little more detail. Then it came to its own conclusions on whether a trust existed or whether the property formed part of the common good of both burghs. No other possibility seems to have been suggested to it in argument.

Although their Lordships took a great deal of time over the discussion of whether the property formed some form of separate trust, that issue may be dealt with fairly briefly here. The surrounding correspondence and, indeed, the wording of the disposition itself, clearly showed an intention on the part of the Duke of Fife to give the property off as a gift and not in trust. Their Lordships held that property could form part of the common good of both burghs, and that the peculiar wording of the joint destination did not, of itself, create a trust.

The main point of interest in the case is not, however, in relation to whether or not the disposition formed part of a trust. It was fairly clear from the facts and circumstances that it did not. The important point of the case for present purposes is that their Lordships, in considering what the property might otherwise be classified as, determined that it could *only* therefore form part of the common good of the burgh. Lord Mackay, in the course of a long judgment, said:

> "[Burghs] are endowed from their origin with certain gifts of land or, it may be, other endowments, but they also are clothed with certain rights or monopolies, and with powers to stent both the citizens and those who enter their grounds for trade. The property rights of all sorts are common good; the powers to stent and the rest are rights not forming part of the common good[8]. I know of, and after extensive search have found, no third or intermediate kind of right originally effeiring to Royal Burghs other than these two. Statutes have in various ways added duties, such as provision of water or streets or light, and have with the duties conferred various additional powers to raise 'rates' for these special or other

8 At 379.

general municipal purposes. Revenues or others relative to these
rates are not 'common good'. The broad distinction has run on and
still runs at this date. It must lastly be said that the ancient authorities make it clear that 'accessions' to the original property endowments, whether emanating from the Sovereign or from the
wealthy landowners who set up the Burgh of Barony in their lands
or other endowers, were contemplated. It is matter of the clearest
assumption in decision after decision that such 'accessions' are contemplated, and when accepted fall into and form part of the
common good."[9]

His Lordship then goes on to concede that section 97 of the
1900 Act makes allowance for one other type of burgh property,
that of property held by a burgh as trustee for any "charity,
foundation, or mortification".

This passage, taken on its own, is likely to be somewhat alarm-
ing for the modern-day conveyancer faced with the sale of any
heritable property originally within the ownership of a burgh. It
seems to suggest that the whole lot forms part of the common
good. Although statutory powers are mentioned by Lord Mackay,
he does not appear to suggest that the use of statutory powers could
give rise to any other classification of burgh property. Lord Wark,
the next judge to give his opinion, differs slightly. He says, much
more succinctly:

". . . there was in the end no dispute between the parties that all
property of a Royal Burgh or a Burgh of Barony not acquired
under statutory powers or held under special trusts forms part of
the common good"[10].

A similar approach is adopted by Lord Jamieson. He says:

"Parliament has been careful to prescribe for the preparation and
audit of annual accounts of Town Council's intromissions with the
whole of the property and revenue of burghs. These fall under the
heads of common good, assessments, revenue-producing subjects
held under statutory powers, and charities or mortifications the
management of which is vested in the council as sole trustees. It

9 See **4.1** for a discussion of this point.
10 At 384.

appears to me that the Duff House estate can only be placed in the first of these categories."[11]

The Lord Justice-Clerk, Lord Cooper, mainly confines himself to a few observations on the topic of joint property which seems to have exercised their Lordships far more than the question at issue here. He does say:

"Special considerations would, of course, apply to a case in which, by the express terms of a disposition or deed of gift to a burgh, the granter had impressed the transfer with specific conditions affecting the management, control or use of the subjects – a result of which, in this instance, the pursuer strove to attain but failed – for subjects so transferred and accepted might not fall into common good. But that is not this case. For the reasons given by your Lordships, I consider that the theory of trust advanced by the pursuers has completely failed (a) because there was no effective separation of the legal title from the beneficial right and (b) because there are no distinctive trust purposes."[12]

This does not really take matters any further forward on the question of what constitutes common good title, although it does have relevance for later cases, examined shortly in **5.2**. The reader is left, therefore, with three judgments which, taken together, seem to suggest that all burgh property, in so far as it has not been acquired using statutory powers or forms part of separate trust estate administered by burghs, must form part of the common good of the burgh.

It seems that the *Ruthin Castle* case is the first time questions of burgh property and common good were looked at in this way. The *Murray* case, discussed in so much detail in chapter 4, and its classifications of common good property, are in reality concerned with common good property which is of a character that renders it incapable of being alienated because the public have rights to it, either by the actings of the authority, by public use, or by dedication in the title.

The *Ruthin Castle* case, because of the peculiar nature of its facts,

11 At 387.
12 At 387.

dealt with a different question. There was no dispute between the parties that, if the property fell into the common good at all, then because of the provisions of section 98 of the Town Councils (Scotland) Act 1900, the magistrates of both burghs should have advertised the lease for public roup instead of coming to a private bargain with the original tenants. The string of nineteenth-century cases regarding alienability were not referred to by counsel for either side or the judges because they did not consider them relevant. All that mattered was whether the property was held in a special trust or not; and, if not, then both sides in the case seemed to have accepted that it would have fallen into the common good.

However, although it is easy enough to follow the reasoning in the *Ruthin Castle* case, and see that it is not entirely at conflict with the nineteenth-century cases such as *Murray*, the case still presents some difficulties. Instead of producing a narrow set of classifications in terms of usage of properties, it challenges the conveyancer to look at the purposes for which property has been acquired. It also runs against what appears to be the understanding of many burghs in so far as their accounting practices do not disclose the vast majority of burgh property to be held on the common good account. This could be seen earlier in the *Cockenzie and Port Seton*[13] case, where East Lothian District Council tried to argue, unsuccessfully, that just because the property in question was not reflected in the common good accounts of the former burgh, this was indicative that it did not fall into the common good.

5.3   Case law following *Ruthin Castle*

Several more recent cases have followed, at least in part, the reasoning advanced by their Lordships in the *Ruthin Castle* case. In *Cockenzie and Port Seton Community Council v East Lothian District Council*[14], Lord Osborne said:

13 1997 SLT 81.
14 1997 SLT 81.

"My consideration of the authorities which were cited in relation to the criterion by which the question of whether property is common good is to be decided, suggests that the matter is not free from difficulty. It is possible to find propositions couched in the broadest terms to the effect that the common good of a burgh consists of the entire property of the burgh, which is held by the corporation for behoof of the community . . . a similar broad view of the matter was taken by Lord Wark in *Magistrates of Banff v Ruthin Castle Limited.*"

Lord Osborne then goes on to quote the passage from Lord Wark referred to above, to the effect that:

"All property of a Royal Burgh or a Burgh of Barony not acquired under statutory powers or held under special trusts forms part of the common good."

Lord Osborne also refers to the dicta of Lord Cooper referred to above but reaches the conclusion that he should follow the "broad approach" of Lord Wark. He goes on to say:

"I am confirmed in that view by the passage in para 1250 of Volume 2 of *Green's Encyclopaedia* to the effect that the class of common good property usually consists of public lands or buildings, such as churches, town halls, market places and common greens or grounds set apart for the general use or enjoyment of the inhabitants."

He then goes on to quote with approval the phrase used by Lord Wylie in the case of *Waddell v Stewartry District Council*[15] that common good property was that which "by custom or dedication by direct grant" the community was entitled to have. In the case before him, of course, there was a "dedication by direct grant" for use as a swimming pool and associated offices.

It is also worth noting that Lord Osborne, whilst not expressly disapproving of the opinion of Lord Cooper in the *Ruthin Castle* case, states that he would not be "confident in giving effect to the tentative opinion expressed by Lord Cooper, which I have quoted, simply on the basis of the terms of the Feu Charter involved in this case". In other words, he did not feel that the classification

15 1977 SLT (Notes) 35.

advanced by Lord Cooper was one into which the case before him fell. This seems to bolster the view that the judgments of Lord Wark and Lord Jamieson are to be preferred in the *Ruthin Castle* case on this point.

The *Ruthin Castle* case was also followed in *Fife Council v Leven Community Council*[16]. The case concerned a plant nursery which formed part of the grounds of a property known as Carberry House which had been gifted to the burgh of Leven by a local landowner in 1929. The history of the property was that, in 1929, Sir Robert Balfour made over the subjects to Leven Burgh "as a gift to be used for the general purposes of the town".

The house and grounds had been used for various administrative purposes in connection with the burgh and its successor councils since its acquisition. The particular area of ground in question had been used as a plant nursery since at least 1939. Due to rationalisation of the local authority's plant nurseries, Carberry Nursery had been closed in 2000 as uneconomic.

Ingeniously, if not particularly ingenuously, the petitioners attempted to argue that the property was not part of the common good. The dedication in the title that the property was to be used "for the general purposes of the town" was said to be insufficient to make the land part of the common good, compared with other, more specific dedications to the common good or common good type purposes in other titles. The *Ruthin Castle* case, according to the agent for the petitioners, was another example of a clear dedication to a public purpose in that the house and policies of Duff House were being given over to the two burghs for the public to enjoy a recreational use of them. In this case, the land at Carberry which had been used for a plant nursery had never been dedicated to a "public" use.

Sheriff Keane was not convinced. Quoting with approval the opinions of Lord Mackay and Lord Jamieson in the *Ruthin Castle* case, the sheriff also commented on the terms of Lord Justice-Clerk Cooper's opinion at 387 in that case in relation to special consider-

---

16 Kirkcaldy Sh Ct, 25 July 2001, unreported. The writer has to declare a personal interest here as he was the solicitor who argued the case before Sheriff Keane.

ations applying to a case in which "by the express terms of a dis-position or deed of gift to a burgh, the granter had impressed the transfer with specific conditions affecting the management, control or use of the subjects, since subjects so transferred and accepted might not fall into common good". Sheriff Keane said that he considered that Lord Cooper "had in mind some form of transfer which would exclude the gifted property from the common good; thus the gift of land to build a road, or to provide space for sewage facilities, while these might benefit the community, would not necessarily form part of common good but come within the functions of a burgh in the provision of services".

In the present case, there was no such specific dedication to non-common good type uses and, accordingly, he held that the property did fall within the definition of common good land. Another indicative factor was a witness for the community council who spoke to his understanding that common good funds had been applied to the redecoration of Carberry House, the inference being that the house and land fell into the common good.

Sheriff Keane did not, however, consider that the former plant nursery fell into any of the categories of common good land which were inalienable and allowed the sale. He did impose specific conditions that the sale proceeds be applied to the common good fund, despite an argument from the petitioners that, as the land had not been used for a common good purpose, some or even all of the proceeds should be directed to the council's general fund.

In retrospect, both Sheriff Keane in *Fife Council v Leven Community Council* and Lord Osborne in *Cockenzie and Port Seton* were right in attempting to come to a decision based on a blend of both the *Ruthin Castle* approach to common good classification and the different approach taken by the nineteenth-century cases.

If the judgments in the *Ruthin Castle* case can be taken at their most consistent, then all burgh property falls into the common good with two exceptions: special trusts or gifts with specific anti-common good purposes, and property acquired under statute for statutory purposes. There is also a third possible exception: land which has been dedicated to statutory purposes since its original acquisition.

Where the nineteenth-century cases are really useful is determining whether a quality of inalienability exists in relation to a common good property. This string of case law reached its zenith with *Murray v Magistrates of Forfar*, discussed in detail in chapter 4. This means that the nineteenth-century cases do still come into play when determining questions of alienability or otherwise. The *Ruthin Castle* case, however, does cause local authorities problems in relation to the extent of former burgh property which falls into the common good – and that whether or not they are considering disposing of it. This is because the common good nature of the property will affect the rules by which it is administered, as outlined in chapter 3.

It also begs the question. What is the extent of the exceptions proposed by the *Ruthin Castle* judges? In other words, when is burgh property not common good?

5.4   When is burgh property not common good?

The *Ruthin Castle* approach to classifying all burgh land as common good with certain defined exceptions appears, superficially, to have the advantage of simplicity. However, that depends on the exceptions being defined or definable.

For most purposes, the easiest exclusion is property which the burghs held as trustees for "any charity, foundation or mortification", as defined in section 97 of the Town Councils (Scotland) Act 1900. This separate class has been carried forward through subsequent local authority reorganisations[17] but, for the reasons outlined at **1.4**, and given the reasoning in the *Ruthin Castle* case itself, it is unlikely that this will account for a large amount of burgh property. Where such trusts do exist, they will be fairly well defined and established as separate entities administered by the council as trusts.

It is probably also safe to disregard the words of Lord Cooper in the *Ruthin Castle* case, as interpreted by Lord Osborne in the *Cockenzie and Port Seton* case, where, by the express terms of a disposition or deed of gift to a burgh, the granter had impressed the

---

17 See Local Government etc (Scotland) Act 1994, s 16.

transfer with specific conditions affecting the management, control or use of the subjects. It is not likely that Lord Cooper meant to create a different class of property which was neither a trust nor common good. From the contents of the report, it seems that he was attempting simply to achieve a shorthand for the definition of trust property which his fellow judges had expressed at greater length.

That leaves what might be called the "statutory powers/statutory purposes exemption". That is a rather clumsy name for it but is necessary because the *Ruthin Castle* judges are not of one mind when it comes to this exemption.

Lord Mackay in fact says that the property rights of the burgh are all common good and only talks about statutes in terms of adding duties and powers to raise rates[18].

Lord Wark, it will be recalled, says that: "All property of a Royal Burgh or a Burgh of Barony not acquired under statutory powers or held under special trusts forms part of the common good"[19].

Lord Jamieson, on the other hand, talks about the accounting headings of the property and revenue on burghs and says: "These fall under the heads of common good, assessments, revenue-producing subjects held under statutory powers and charities or mortifications, the management of which is vested in the council as sole trustee"[20].

Lord Cooper does not mention any type of property held by a burgh under statutory powers but says generally that he agrees with the other judges.

What conclusions can be drawn from all of this? Nowadays, all land is technically acquired by local authorities under statutory powers – in general, under section 74 of the Local Government (Scotland) Act 1973, although occasionally under other statutes where an element of compulsion is required – e.g. section 189 of the Town and Country Planning (Scotland) Act 1997. However, the position has not always been as straight-

18 1944 SLT at 379.
19 1944 SLT at 384.
20 1944 SLT at 387.

forward as this, and to fully understand what the judges had in mind – and therefore reach some kind of delineation of this exemption – it is necessary to delve a little deeper into the historical position once again.

The case of *Nicol v Magistrates of Aberdeen*[21] concerned the proposed purchase of a one-half *pro indiviso* share of the estate of Torry by the magistrates. Partly the case was about the propriety of the original decision, which was taken at a meeting where a magistrate with an interest in the other *pro indiviso* share in the estate was present. The petitioners also attacked the right of the magistrates to undertake such a speculative acquisition; but the court refused to interfere with the decision to acquire, stating that it was *intra vires*. This case was accordingly authority for the proposition that authorities could acquire land for common good purposes without any statutory authority.

However, as the nineteenth century progressed, various statutory powers and responsibilities were devolved upon the burghs, and with these powers and responsibilities came the right to acquire land for specific statutory purposes. Mention has been made already of Hutton, in his preface to his commentary on the Local Government (Scotland) Act 1947, noting with approval that it consolidates 178 separate enactments, scattered over the statute book of the previous 120 years. Time and space are not in favour of listing the pieces of legislation which might apply, but the Fourth Schedule to the 1947 Act gives a useful starting list, being enactments not affected by the general provisions for acquisition with the consent of the Secretary of State contained in the 1947 Act itself:

> ➤ the Burial Grounds Acts;
> ➤ the Electricity (Supply) Acts, 1882 to 1936;
> ➤ the Military Lands Acts, 1892 to 1903;
> ➤ the Light Railways Acts, 1896 and 1912;
> ➤ the Cremation Act, 1902;
> ➤ the Housing (Scotland) Acts, 1925 to 1946;

21 (1879) 9 M 306.

> the Restriction of Ribbon Development Act, 1935;
> the Town and Country Planning (Scotland) Act, 1945;
> the Water (Scotland) Act, 1946;
> the Education (Scotland) Act, 1946;
> any local Act.

Obviously, these pieces of legislation are only the Acts which were still in existence at the time of the 1947 Act and will have statutory forebears going back into the nineteenth century. The other source of powers for statutory acquisitions which might be a first reference point for conveyancers trying to establish whether land might have been acquired for a statutory purpose would be the Burgh Police (Scotland) Acts and, in particular, the Burgh Police (Scotland) Act 1892:

> section 108 (cleansing);
> section 154 (improvement of streets/street widening/acquisition of waste/ruinous buildings/improvement/improvement of sanitary conditions of localities);
> section 193 (ruinous buildings again);
> section 261 (waterworks – succeeded by the Water (Scotland) Act 1946);
> section 277 (markets);
> section 278 (slaughterhouses);
> section 291 (fire stations);
> section 307 (pleasure grounds or places of public resort or recreation);
> section 309 (public baths and wash houses, public covered or open bathing places and public drying grounds);
> section 315 (public halls and offices, a court hall, police offices, all public conveniences thereto and police houses).

It is clear from this non-exhaustive list that a very wide range of statutory powers existed for acquisition of property, particularly from the late nineteenth century onwards. Proving what purpose land was acquired for, of course, will not always be straightforward over a hundred years on. The best case scenario is that the burgh in acquiring the property specifically narrated the relevant legislation, following the practice commented on with approval by Hutton in his commentary on the 1947 Act[22].

In the absence of such an express declaration in the title, the modern-day conveyancer is left with the unenviable task of unearthing some type of evidence from ancient minutes or correspondence around the time of the purchase. However, historical evidence that a property was used for something with a statutory purpose such as, for example, a police house, would seem to be *prima facie* evidence that the property was not intended to form part of the common good.

More extreme difficulties of proof will arise, of course, in relation to the types of statutory purpose which could also be said to be common good purposes, such as the provision of public recreation spaces, and there the burden of proof might be said to shift towards showing that the property had not simply fallen into that public use rather than having been specifically acquired under statutory powers using rates income for that purpose. In that context, the ancient nature or otherwise of the title might come into play, and Lord McLaren's dicta on that point in the *Murray* case may acquire particular relevance[23].

It should also be mentioned that, to a limited extent, land may have been appropriated from the common good for a statutory purpose. This is because section 171 of the 1947 Act applies the provision of that part of the Act generally "with respect to the *appropriation*, letting, selling, feuing or excambing of land belonging to a local authority" (writer's italics). The relevant section on appropriation is section 163, which says:

"A local authority may, with consent of the Secretary of State, appropriate for the purpose of any function, whether statutory or otherwise, land vested in them for the purpose of any other function, subject to proper adjustments in respect thereof being made in the accounts of the authority."

Hutton in his commentary suggests that a certified copy of the

---

22 W Hutton, *The Local Government (Scotland) Act 1947* (1949) at 265; see also **2.1**.

23 (1893) 20 R 908 at 920 and see **4.3**.

resolution and also the letter from the Secretary of State should be put with the titles to the land. An appropriation of this nature would seem to be one of the clearest examples of the land in question being no longer part of the common good. However, only common good land with respect to which no question arises as to the right of the council to alienate it could – or at least should – have been appropriated in this way.

What conclusions can be drawn from all of this? Certainly, classifying common good land is no simple task. However, the two strings of case law which at first appear to conflict with each other can more or less be synthesised into one coherent whole.

The starting-point is the later twentieth-century cases and, in particular, the judgments of Lord Jamieson and Lord Wark in the *Ruthin Castle* case. This string of case law starts from the presumption that all burgh property forms part of the common good subject to certain exceptions. Whilst land held in special trust can probably be disregarded as a rarity, the exception relating to land acquired for statutory purposes will, in fact, take quite a lot of former burgh land out of the equation as far as common good is concerned – particularly property acquired from the middle of the nineteenth century onwards.

It may be that, even by rigorous application of this exception, local authorities will find that they have more common good land than they previously thought. Even before considering questions of disposal, this will have consequences for local authorities carrying out a title audit. For reasons explained already, the treatment of individual properties in the accounts of the former burghs will be of limited use[24]. There is really no alternative to carrying out as informed an investigation as is now possible of the circumstances surrounding each acquisition.

Such an audit is likely to mean difficult questions will have to be asked as regards maintenance and repair costs and whether these are to be met by the self-contained common good fund; it will also

---

24 See **4.2**. A recent Opinion of senior counsel suggests that an account of this nature was reflecting only common good properties which might not be capable of alienation, an interpretation which might well have considerable merit.

mean that the receipts from any disposals (and rentals) of property found to be common good should normally be paid into the common good fund.

Having established, by use of the later twentieth-century cases, a broad classification of common good land, the nineteenth-century cases which reach their fullest expression in judgments like those of *Murray v Magistrates of Forfar* can be brought into play. These cases then create a classification within a classification, namely common good land which may be subject to some form of restriction on its disposal. It has been seen that the *Murray* case produces three sub-classifications: land and buildings which, by use by the public from time immemorial, have acquired that character; land or buildings dedicated to some form of public purpose by the burgh itself; and deeds of gift by benefactors which expressly dedicate the subjects to a common good purpose. The shorthand for this in the judgments is "custom, dedication, or direct grant".

Appendix IV provides a simplified schematic of the process authorities require to go through to establish whether a former burgh property is (a) part of the common good, and (b) part of that sub-group of common good property in respect of which a question arises as to the right of the authority to alienate.

The next question for consideration is the vexed one of when, and in what circumstances, a local authority can dispose of, alienate, or appropriate, common good property.

Chapter 6

Appropriation, alienation and disposal of common good land

6.1 Appropriation, alienation and disposal

In **2.2** it was shown that the principal area of common good law which is subject to legislative control is the disposal of land[1] and that the extant provisions of the Local Government (Scotland) Act 1973 still hold sway. It was also clear that section 75 of that Act, which deals with disposal of land forming part of the common good, forms part of a suite of provisions relating to acquisition, appropriation and disposal of land by local authorities. For ease of reference, the text of the section is reproduced again here:

> "**75. Disposal, etc, of land forming part of the common good**
>
> (1) The provisions of this Part of this Act with respect to the **appropriation** or **disposal** of land belonging to a local authority shall apply in the case of land forming part of the common good of an authority with respect to which land no question arises as to the right of the authority to **alienate**.
>
> (2) Where a local authority desire to **dispose** of land forming part of the common good with respect to which land a question arises as to the right of the authority to **alienate**, they may apply to the Court of Session or the Sheriff to authorise them to **dispose** of the land, and the Court or Sheriff may, if they think fit, authorise the authority to **dispose** of the land subject to such conditions, if any, as they may impose, and the authority shall be entitled to **dispose** of land accordingly.
>
> (3) The Court of Session or Sheriff acting under subsection (2) above may impose a condition requiring that the local auth-

---

1 "Land" is taken to comprehend any interest in land, and therefore buildings: see Local Government (Scotland) Act 1973, s 235.

ority shall provide in substitution for the land proposed to be **disposed** of other land to be used for the same purpose for which the former land was used."

In the text, the three words in bold type relate to what a local authority might want to do with land. At first sight, they appear to be used interchangeably. In fact, they mean very different things. To a certain extent, particularly in the case of disposal, their meaning has been judicially considered. It is absolutely crucial to the understanding of the exact effect of section 75 – the central statutory provision affecting any dealings in common good land – that the full nuances of the three words are understood. There are, of course, other words and phrases in the section that need to be looked at and that task will be undertaken shortly: however, the starting-point to understanding of the section is to consider alienation, appropriation and disposal.

Alienation

Alienation is the word which is used most frequently in the case law concerning common good properties. It is used in the *Murray* case[2] which concerned a proposed ten-year lease. It is used in the case of *Crawford v Magistrates of Paisley*[3], a case concerning the taking down of a steeple. It can be seen right away, therefore, that the term does not necessarily mean the same as outright disposal to a third party of the property.

There are no other references to alienation outwith section 75 in the 1973 Act and it is not a term which modern legislators favour in relation to conveyancing matters.

Appropriation

Appropriation, on the other hand, has its own section in the 1973 Act, namely section 73. It states that, subject to certain exceptions, a local authority may appropriate, for the purpose of any function, whether statutory or otherwise, land vested in it for the purpose

---

2 *Murray v Magistrates of Forfar* (1893) 20 R 908, (1893) 1 SLT 105.
3 (1870) 8 M 693.

of any other such function (subsection (1)); it may not do this for land held as use for allotments without the consent of the Secretary of State[4] (subsections (2) and (3)). Appropriation, therefore, has a relatively clear meaning. It means a local authority using common good land for another function but not transferring it out of its ownership.

Disposal

Like appropriation, disposal has its own specific section in the 1973 Act, namely section 74. This provides that the local authority may dispose of land held by it in any manner it wishes, subject to the best consideration requirements already examined in **2.2**. Disposal is nowhere defined in this section, nor in section 75, nor, indeed, anywhere else in the Act. However, it is freely used in other statutes[5] and is generally held to mean transfer out of the hands of the local authority, whether by means of disposition, lease or something that gives a third party ascertainable rights of beneficial occupation. This is to be contrasted with the meaning of alienation, which in the context of the common good cases, is generally approached from the point of view of interfering with the rights of the inhabitants of the burgh and not whether or not a third party is necessarily gaining rights.

On this analysis, the following interpretation of section 75(1) seems to be reasonable:

> ➢ A local authority may appropriate any common good land, with respect to which no question arises as to the right of the authority to alienate, for the purpose of any other function, statutory or otherwise (sections 73(1) and 75(1) taken together).

> ➢ A local authority may dispose of common good land with respect to which no question arises as to the right of the authority to alienate for best consideration (section 74(1)) or

---

4 Now the Scottish Ministers.

5 See, eg, the Town and Country Planning (Scotland) Act 1997, s 191 and the Housing (Scotland) Act 1987, ss 9 and 10.

for less than best consideration (section 74(2)) without reference to the court.

➢ Where a local authority desires to dispose of common good land where a question does arise as to the authority's right to alienate that land, it requires to go to court for authority.

➢ A local authority cannot, *at least in so far as section 75 is concerned*, appropriate common good land to another purpose where a question arises as to its ability to alienate. Nor can it apply to the court under section 75 to do so.

➢ A local authority cannot, *at least in terms of section 75*, alienate such common good land in a manner which falls short of disposal.

These last two statements in particular may seem at first controversial but they are made solely on the basis of straightforward construction of the provisions of section 75 making the reasonable assumption that the legislative draftsman, in using appropriation, alienation and disposal in different parts of the section, was doing so knowingly and purposefully and with a view to precision of meaning. Leaving aside until the next chapter the issue of when a question arises as to the authority's right to alienate, it is useful to examine some cases concerning the more straightforward issue of disposal before turning again to look at the more vexed questions of appropriations and alienations falling short of disposal.

6.2 Disposal of common good land

There are numerous examples of cases dealing with what would commonly be understood by conveyancers as a "disposal", ie outright transfer of title or a lease of some kind. Examples can be found in *Murray v Magistrates of Forfar*[6] (ten-year lease); *Magistrates of Kirkcaldy v Marks & Spencer Ltd*[7] (outright sale); and even short-term leases, in the case of *Blackie v Magistrates of Edinburgh*[8].

---

6 (1893) 20 R 908, (1893) 1 SLT 105.
7 1937 SLT 574.
8 (1884) 11 R 783.

However, the clearest expression of what constitutes a disposal for the purposes of the 1973 Act is that contained in *East Lothian District Council v National Coal Board*[9]. This case will be discussed in much more detail in relation to the issue of when a question arises. However, for present purposes, it can be noted that the case was an application under section 75(2) to grant a ninety-nine-year lease of land at Musselburgh.

Lord Maxwell, sitting as Lord Ordinary, discussed, first, the concept of alienation at common law, noting that a ten-year lease in the *Murray* case was treated as an alienation, as also the three-week concession for a fisheries exhibition in the *Blackie* case, although he clearly doubted the strength of the latter authority[10]. Having considered the common law, Lord Maxwell then went on to consider section 75 and noted that the provisions are a re-enactment (with some alterations and simplification of wording)[11] of the provisions in section 171 of the 1947 Act. He then said:

> "In the 1973 provisions, what the court is empowered to authorise is 'disposal' and I think it clear that 'dispose' includes letting as well as selling and feuing. Section 173 of the 1947 Act shows that the word 'dispose' is intended to include disposal by lease."[12]

If a local authority desires to sell a common good property or to lease it for any substantial period, then the provisions of section 75(1) and (2) come into play[13]. Another relatively common requirement, however, is for a property forming part of the common good to be demolished. Whether or not that constitutes disposal for the purposes of section 75 is a slightly more difficult question.

---

9 1982 SLT 460.

10 At 467: "I think that that case perhaps involves rather different considerations".

11 At 468.

12 At 468.

13 Possibly with the crucial exception of leases with a lease-back arrangement to the authority: see the discussion of *South Lanarkshire, Petitioners* at **6.4**.

6.3   Demolition

Two cases, a hundred years apart, deal with the issue of demolition. Although the first of these can give confidence that demolition of a common good property constitutes alienation, the second of them is only tentative authority for the proposition that it constitutes disposal under the 1973 Act.

In *Crawford v Magistrates of Paisley*[14] the magistrates had decided to demolish the steeple belonging to the burgh for the purposes of road widening. Mr Crawford successfully interdicted the magistrates from carrying out demolition on this basis. However, it was subsequently found that the building was a danger to life and property and the magistrates successfully had the interdict recalled on that basis.

In determining the question of expenses for the interdict action, in the Inner House, the Lord President and Lord Deas expressed their opinions on the propriety of the magistrates having sought to demolish the building without judicial authority.

The Lord President said:

"It must be observed that this steeple is not only the public property of the burgh, but it is inalienable property. They could not sell it and, most unquestionably, they could just as little pull it down without judicial authority, unless the immediate risk was so imminent as to entitle them, for the safety of the community, to do so."[15]

Lord Deas said:

"As your Lordship has observed, this steeple was part of the inalienable property of the burgh, which they could not sell, and could not take down, except on necessity."[16]

These dicta were quoted with approval in *Waddell v Stewartry District Council*[17]. This case concerned very similar facts and circumstances to *Crawford*. Stewartry District Council proposed to de-

14 (1870) 8 M 693.
15 At 696.
16 At 697.
17 1977 SLT (Notes) 35.

molish the town hall and associated buildings at Gatehouse of Fleet and a ratepayer sought interdict against them on the basis that the property was part of the inalienable part of the common good, with a title condition to the effect that two-thirds of the ratepayers of the burgh had to consent to its "disposal".

This is one of the first cases to have come before the court after the passing of the 1973 Act and it is unfortunate for present purposes that the case was complicated by the specific title condition and its format as an interdict action. However, Lord Wylie took the view that the issues in relation to the title condition and the interpretation of section 75 of the 1973 Act gave rise to the same question, ie whether the proposed demolition of the building constituted alienation or disposal of the subjects at all.

Quoting, with approval, the judgments of Lord President Inglis and Lord Deas in the *Crawford* case just referred to, Lord Wylie said:

> "I have accordingly come to the view that, in this context, what constitutes alienation must be liberally construed and would include any action which effectively deprives the community of something which, by custom or dedication by direct grant, they are entitled to have. If an authority cannot deprive their community of the use of property which is inalienable by disposing of it in the ordinary commercial sense of the term, or by making a gift of it, it would only be in accordance with the underlying principle that they could not deprive the community of its use by destroying it, except in the highly special circumstance of imminent danger to the public. In the context of the deed itself, . . . I shall consider that a similarly wide construction falls to be placed on the words 'dispose of'."[18]

So far as section 75 is concerned, Lord Wylie was much more cautious. He said:

> "As to whether the same words where they appear in section 75 of the 1973 Act fall to be similarly construed, I express no view. These provisions were not canvassed in argument in any detail and notwithstanding the wide terms of section 74(1) may well be that

in the statutory context, disposal of land is envisaged only in a commercial sense. The previous statutory provision, namely, section 171 of the 1947 Act, would seem to relate to the selling and feuing of land but the group of sections in that Act relating to the disposal of land generally is very different and much more specific than the way in which this is treated in the 1973 Act."[19]

Accordingly, although it can be said with confidence from these two cases that demolition of common good property constitutes an alienation, it is not absolutely clear-cut that demolition can be treated as a disposal for the purposes of the Act. Lord Wylie has a point when he says that "disposal", in the context of the 1973 Act and the general disposal provisions of section 74, might be construed in a broader sense. However, the safest way to proceed with a derelict common good property requiring demolition, at least so far as a local authority is concerned, would be for it to be advertised for sale with the purchaser carrying out the demolition. That way, the action brought to the court can be on surer ground when it talks about disposal. That seems to have been the thinking behind the actings of the petitioners in the *Stirling District Council* case[20].

In reality, whether or not *Waddell* is authority for demolition counting as disposal for the purposes of the 1973 Act, in most cases where demolition is desired, the local authority will want to include in the action a conclusion for subsequent disposal of the property. In most instances where that is not the case, the reason for the demolition is likely to be that the building is dangerous in terms of the Building (Scotland) Act 2003 and, in that instance, it would appear to be accepted that a council could proceed to have the building demolished by following the provisions of that legislation.

So much for demolition, which has its own solutions to gaps left by the case law. It is necessary to now turn to consider a more difficult set of circumstances, thrown into relief by a recent case.

19 At 36.
20 Outer House, 19 May 2000, unreported: available on www.scotcourts. gov.uk and see **8.1**.

6.4 Appropriations/alienations falling short of disposal

In **6.1** it became clear that the text of section 75 of the 1973 Act used the words alienation, appropriation and disposal in quite a precise way. It also became clear that, where what the authority proposed did not amount to a disposal but was still an alienation or appropriation of some form, section 75 did not provide the authority with a remedy for defeating the common law principle that such alienations or appropriations could not proceed if the property formed part of the inalienable part of the common good.

Arguably, some of the old cases are examples of such a situation. In *Paterson v Magistrates of St Andrews*[21], a case examined in **4.3**, what was proposed was really an appropriation by the magistrates of part of the land at the side of the golf links for the construction of a road. They were not proposing to actually dispose of the *solum* of the road to anyone else. Indeed, in their interlocutor, their Lordships made it a condition of agreeing to the proposal that no such disposal took place.

In *Grahame v Magistrates of Kirkcaldy*[22], on the other hand, what could be construed as an appropriation was refused by the court. An area of land which had been part of the common muir had fallen into disuse and the magistrates, who were also the police commissioners of the burgh, proposed to build police stables on the land. Admittedly, they also proposed to dispone the land to themselves as police commissioners, but the action was brought against them as magistrates and as police commissioners not just to interdict the granting of the disposition but also to interdict them from "applying" the land to "any purpose inconsistent with [the] common use and enjoyment"[23].

This case will appear again in **8.1** in the context of an authority pleading its own neglect. However, for now, it can be seen that their Lordships' decision was based not just on the proposed disposition but also on the fundamental question of whether the

21 (1880) 7 R 712, (1881) 8 R (HL) 117.
22 (1879) 6 R 1066.
23 At 1067.

burgh had the right "to deal with the ground in question in any way inconsistent with the right of the inhabitants"[24].

In reality, there is not a great difference between the concept of appropriation and that of alienation falling short of disposal so far as the pre-1947 Act and 1973 Act cases are concerned. What was important was that the rights of the inhabitants of the burgh were being limited by the proposed use in some way.

The law may have rested at that point for some time, had it not been for a much more recent decision and one which, perhaps, leaves more questions asked than answered. This is the case of *South Lanarkshire Council, Petitioners*[25], which is particularly difficult to interpret as there was no formal written judgment.

The subject-matter of the case concerned a set of facts and circumstances which will be familiar to many local authorities in the present day. It was proposed to use part of a public park in Hamilton, gifted by the Duke of Hamilton to the then burgh, for the development of a new secondary school using the public/ private partnership ("PPP") delivery method.

As was outlined in **1.4**, the terms of the title from the Duke of Hamilton gave rise to a question as to whether the land was intended to be held in trust by the burgh or whether it fell into the common good. In fact, this was the question that most exercised the petitioners before the case went to court and Opinion was obtained from a conveyancing professor as well as from counsel before the case was brought to court. Professor Rennie was asked only in relation to the trust/common good issue and it is fair to say that counsel concerned himself principally with that point also. However, the petitioners were in for a surprise when the case was considered at a hearing on the summar roll before the Inner House (Lord President Cullen, Lord Eassie and Lady Smith).

The assumption of the petitioners had been, standing the trust/ common good issue, that if the property was considered to be common good then an application for authority of the court under

---

24 At 1075 per Lord Ormidale.
25 Inner House, 11 August 2004, unreported.

section 75(2) of the 1973 Act was necessary because the PPP delivery mechanism was likely at that time to involve a lease of the school site to a private sector partner for a period of thirty years with a corresponding lease-back of the school to the authority. Associated with this would be a services contract between the authority and the private sector partner in terms of which the partner would be obliged to maintain the school buildings during the period of the lease and lease-back.

The assumption that this arrangement constituted a disposal under section 75 was not unreasonable. There were, for example, the precedents of the *East Lothian District Council v National Coal Board*[26] and *Murray v Forfar Magistrates*[27] cases, both of which had involved leases.

However, in the course of the hearing, the judges, *ex proprio motu*, raised a question as to whether the PPP proposal was actually a "disposal" as envisaged by section 75. Noting the possibility that the subjects would be leased to the private sector partner and contemporaneously sub-leased back to the council; that the land would remain in community use albeit a different use than at present; that the school would be occupied by the authority; that there was no commercial purpose involved[28]; that no land was being sold off at this location; and that section 75 had been drafted long before the advent of public/private partnerships, the court gave a strong hint to counsel for the petitioners that if the petitioners were to suggest that this particular use of common good land was not a disposal, it would agree with them.

After the lunch break, counsel for the petitioners went back into court and argued just that. Unsurprisingly, the Inner House accepted the proposition that it did not count as a disposal and an interlocutor to that effect was duly pronounced. Formally, the prayer of the petition was refused as unnecessary "in respect that it is accepted by counsel for the petitioners that the arrangement proposed does not involve a 'disposal' of land for

---

26 1982 SLT 460.
27 (1893) 20 R 908, (1893) 1 SLT 105.
28 That is, presumably, on the part of the local authority.

the purposes of section 75(2) of the Local Government (Scotland) Act 1973"[29].

Whilst the outcome in this case might at first blush appear to be a victory for the local authority, there may be something of a sting in the tail. The court was prepared to determine that the petition was unnecessary in terms of section 75(2) of the 1973 Act. However, given what has been said above in relation to the differences between the cases dealing with alienation at common law and the provisions in section 75(2) relating to disposal, it may well be that an arrangement of this nature might constitute an alienation at common law whilst still not meeting the tests required of it to constitute a disposal for the purposes of section 75(2). And that, perhaps, is taking the court's decision relating to the disposal issue at its very highest.

This view is bolstered by an Opinion of counsel given to another council which the writer has had sight of, in relation to preparations for an application to court for a similar PPP scheme for former playing fields. When news of the Inner House decision on South Lanarkshire's petition broke, the other authority sought advice. Without criticising the decision or the way it had been presented, but concentrating solely on whether it represented a precedent that might be followed, counsel made the following points:

> "that details of the lease and lease-back in the South Lanarkshire case did not appear to have been presented to court and that not all such arrangements were similar;

> "that the petition was unopposed and there is no indication that critical passages in the *East Lothian Council v National Coal Board* case were cited and considered by the court; in particular, the passage at 467 to the effect that even a lease by which the local authority retained some control of the ground by means of conditions was still an alienation at common law on account of the possibility of future unforeseen circumstances;

---

29 A recent case before Lord Drummond Young seems to have come to similar conclusions in similar circumstances. However, at time of going to press no written judgment was available: *North Lanarkshire Council, Petitioners*, 7 Oct 2005.

"that, even if control of the ground was not lost by the council, the use of the land would still be irrevocably changed."

Counsel then went on to suggest that the only safe way to proceed would be to present a petition under section 75(2) coupled with a declarator that, at common law, there is no disposal or unlawful alienation under the proposed arrangement. He made the point, however, that there may be procedural difficulties in doing so in the Court of Session.

One other point occurs, which might be of assistance to authorities in this situation. In **2.3**, mention was made of section 20(1) of the Local Government in Scotland Act 2003, which provides:

"A local authority has power to do anything which it considers is likely to promote or improve the well-being of –
(a) its area and persons within that area; or
(b) either of those."

This provision is the nearest local authorities have ever had to a general dispensing power. It does not affect disposals or appropriations caught by section 75 of the 1973 Act, because these constitute limiting provisions for the purposes of the 2003 Act (section 22). But it does, arguably, cover appropriations or alienations falling short of disposal.

The argument on the part of an authority might be to the effect that, in carrying out an alienation such as a demolition of a derelict building, or a lease and lease-back arrangement for a PPP school, it was doing a thing which *it considers* is likely to promote or improve the well-being of its area and/or persons within that area. Note that the test is not whether, objectively, well-being is advanced, but whether the authority considers it is. Questions of whether any reasonable authority could consider a specific proposal to advance well-being go back to the judicial review cases considered in **3.1**.

It is now time to move on to the last of the fundamental questions to be addressed in considering disposal of common good land. When, for the purposes of section 75 of the 1973 Act, does a question arise as to the ability of a local authority to dispose?

Chapter 7

When does "a question" arise?

7.1 The arising question and the court's discretion

In chapter 6, the wording of section 75 of the Local Government (Scotland) Act 1973 was seen, like its statutory ancestor, section 171 of the 1947 Act, to have been very carefully drafted as regards its uses of the words appropriation, alienation and disposal.

One phrase in section 75 – which again it inherited from section 171 of the 1947 Act – needs to be interpreted for a full understanding of what the section might mean. This is the phrase "land forming part of the common good with respect to which land a question arises as to the right of the authority to alienate". It occurs in section 75(1) and (2) and its true meaning will clearly have an effect on whatever an authority has in mind in relation to common good land, whether it be appropriation, alienation or disposal. What, then, does it mean?

It is no coincidence that the phrase first appeared in the 1947 Act. In an earlier chapter[1], it was seen that the legislators appeared to have been influenced in their drafting of section 171 by *Magistrates of Kirkcaldy v Marks & Spencer Ltd*[2] in putting in a subsection, removed as redundant in the 1973 Act, about former burgh chambers. In the same way, it would seem that the legislators were influenced by the *Ruthin Castle*[3] case, and its dicta that almost all burgh land and buildings fell into the common good. They seem to have recognised, however, that only some properties raised questions as to the ability of the authority to alienate them: namely

1 See **2.1**.
2 1937 SLT 574.
3 *Magistrates of Banff v Ruthin Castle Ltd* 1944 SC 36, 1944 SLT 373.

those properties which fell into the type of categories discussed in *Murray v Magistrates of Forfar*[4].

On the face of things, that interpretation makes sense. If the land has a title dedicating it to a public purpose; if it has been dedicated to a public purpose by the authority; or if the public has, without hindrance by the authority, used the property for public purposes such as recreation on it, then a question could be said to arise. If none of the above applies, then no question arises and the authority may safely deal with the common good land as it pleases.

That may advance matters a little, but there will still be borderline cases where it would appear to the authority to be safe to proceed without reference to the Court of Session or the sheriff but, perhaps, members of the community disagree. What then? How could no question be said to arise when there is (often) a very public disagreement over the public authority's ability to dispose of the land?

Although the case law is not very helpful on this point, there are some useful judicial comments. In *Cockenzie and Port Seton Community Council v East Lothian District Council*[5], a case discussed earlier[6], the community council petitioned the court for judicial review on the basis that East Lothian, by failing to seek authority of the court to dispose of the land under section 75(2), was acting *ultra vires*.

Whilst Lord Osborne said that he had "little difficulty in concluding that . . . it can properly be said that 'a question arises as to the right of the authority to alienate' "[7], he took the view that the subjects had been inalienable when they were fully in use but that, now alternative premises had been made available, the buildings were capable of alienation.

It has already been seen that Lord Osborne also took the view that a local authority's decision to proceed in this way was not in itself *ultra vires*:

"If a local authority desire to dispose of land forming part of the

---

4 (1893) 20 R 908.
5 1997 SLT 81.
6 See **3.2**, **3.3**, **5.1** and **5.3**.
7 1997 SLT at 90.

common good, with respect to which land a question arises as to
the right of the authority to alienate, it appears to me that the local
authority may, if they think fit, no doubt after having taken
appropriate advice, proceed upon a view which commends itself
to them to the effect that they have the right to alienate. In the
event of their doing that, they are of course exposed to the risk that
others may take the view that they do not possess the right to
alienate. In that event, proceedings such as these proceedings may
be brought against them. In such proceedings, it appears to me that
the true question which then arises is whether in fact the property
is or is not inalienable. In other words, the question referred to in
section 75(2) of the Act of 1973 requires to be resolved in such a
situation . . . before the petitioners could succeed in this petition,
they would require to demonstrate positively that the subjects concerned were, at the time of the decision criticised, inalienable."[8]

Lord Osborne quoted two previous cases with approval. The
first of these was *East Lothian District Council v National Coal Board*[9].
That case contains the fullest discussion of any of this issue. However, it arose in the context of a rather ingenious argument by
counsel for the community council.

The subject-matter of the case was Musselburgh Links. The links
had already been the subject of an earlier case, that of *Sanderson v
Lees*[10], discussed earlier at **4.3**. In that case, the burgesses were successful in interdicting the burgh and a builder from developing part
of the links, as the immemorial use of the inhabitants was established.

The ingenious argument advanced by counsel for the community council in the *East Lothian District Council v National Coal
Board* case was this. As the links had been the subject-matter of a
previous alienation case, no question arose as to the ability of the
authority to alienate the land. No question arose because it was
clear that the authority could not alienate the land. As a result, the
district council was, he argued, unable to bring a petition under
section 75(2) of the 1973 Act which only dealt with land where the

8 1997 SLT at 90.
9 1982 SLT 460.
10 (1859) 22 D 24.

question of the ability of the authority to alienate was unresolved. Accordingly, the petition under section 75(2) was incompetent.

Lord Maxwell found some attractions in this argument. Amongst other things, he said:

> "[I]t is by no means clear in what circumstances it is to be said that 'a question arises'. Is it enough that some person, however mistakenly or even capriciously, has raised a question and what is the procedure if the local authority wishes to maintain that there is no question? At one point in the earlier debate, counsel for the petitioner suggested that the present petition might be refused 'as unnecessary', but I do not think that that procedure, often used in trust petitions, is suitable for dealing with substantial rights of this kind. I suppose a local authority could raise a declarator that 'no question arises' and accordingly it has power under s 75(1), but it would be a somewhat odd procedure."[11]

Nevertheless, Lord Maxwell felt he had to sustain a broader construction of the statute:

> "In my opinion, for better or worse, Parliament has conferred on the court a wide and unfettered discretion to authorise disposal where common good land has the quality of inalienability or where it appears that it may have that quality. In exercise of that discretion, I think it right, first, to assume that, if it were to be resolved, the question of inalienability would be resolved in favour of the inhabitants and, second, to have in mind the nature of the inhabitants' common law rights on that assumption."[12]

This approach was followed in *Kirkcaldy District Council v Burntisland Community Council*[13], the second case quoted with approval by Lord Osborne in the *Cockenzie and Port Seton* case. In the *Kirkcaldy* case, Lord Caplan said:

> "I respectfully agree with Lord Maxwell in *East Lothian District Council* that the power of the court to apply section 75(2) should not be regarded too narrowly. Clearly, the alienability of the land in the present case is at least open to argument and I consider there-

---

11 1982 SLT at 469.
12 1982 SLT at 469.
13 1993 SLT 753.

fore that it would be appropriate to grant authority under section 75(2) if the circumstances otherwise justified this."[14]

Some conclusions, then, can be drawn from the case law. A question can be said to arise even if previous case law has found the same piece of land to be incapable of alienation. The court has a wide discretion to consider whether a question arises. The decision of an authority not to take the matter to court will not normally in itself be *ultra vires* but it will be open for others to challenge that decision. Finally, it would be preferable if a petition under section 75(2) were not to be dismissed as being unnecessary.

It might be useful to consider the effect of the section and such judicial commentary as there is on this phrase in the context of some of the typical common good types of property already examined. It might also be useful to approach the issue from both directions. In other words, when can a question be said to arise, and when does it not arise?

7.2   When does a question arise?

The types of land and property which, it would seem, may give rise to a question as to the right of the authority to alienate them may seem to be much larger than the opposite category where no such question might arise. This may be taking too cautious an approach. On the other hand, the consequences of disposing of common good land and then finding that a court considers that a question does arise are, as will be seen, at the very least unclear. It is probably safer, therefore, to apply the *Murray* categories[15] with a fair degree of rigour.

Cases concerning land which has already been the subject of judicial consideration

In *East Lothian District Council v National Coal Board*, discussed above at **7.1**, two interpretations were placed on the fact that Mussel-

14 At 757.
15 See chapter 4.

burgh Links had been the subject of earlier judicial consideration in *Sanderson v Lees*. Counsel for the Musselburgh and Inveresk Community Council argued that the existence of a previous case preventing alienation meant that no question arose as the land was unquestionably incapable of alienation. Counsel for the petitioners, on the other hand, pointed out material differences in the land involved, particularly as some of the land had been reclaimed since 1859 so that the subject of the petition was not exactly the same as the Links had been in 1859.

In the event, Lord Maxwell considered that the court had a broad discretion to determine these matters even if previous case law seemed to have put the matter beyond question. Given the plethora of previous common good decisions – particularly in the nineteenth century – it is possible that a set of circumstances such as the *East Lothian* case will come up again. In that event, it would be prudent to assume that a question arose and to take the matter to court – whatever the previous case had decided.

Title wording

In almost all cases where the burgh's title has contained words of grant which impress it with a common good character, a question is likely to arise as to the right of the authority to alienate that land. Even seemingly innocuous wording, such as "a gift to be used for the general purposes of the town" gave rise to a question as to the right of the authority to alienate[16].

Dedication to public use by the authority

Again, it seems likely that in many cases the use of a public building or area of land which has had a "public" purpose is likely to give rise to a question as to whether an authority can now alienate it – even if a replacement has already been found. An example of this is the *Cockenzie and Port Seton Community Council v East Lothian District Council* case[17] discussed above. An exception might be

16 *Fife Council, Petitioners* Kirkcaldy Sh Ct, 25 July 2001, unreported.
17 1997 SLT 81.

where a public building has long since ceased to have its public use, but, unless an alternative use has been found, authorities would have to be careful that there was no issue of the authority pleading its own neglect[18], in which case, a question would undoubtedly arise.

Use from time immemorial by the public itself

Most cases relating to use from time immemorial will be dealing with disputed facts. It is hard to see how a question could not be held to arise – even if the authority were subsequently successful. See, for example, the case of *Montgomerie v Wallace-James*[19], where an allegation of common good use by the inhabitants of the burgh was successfully repelled, but only after an extensive proof and appeal to the House of Lords.

7.3 When does a question not arise?

Whilst the class of properties which falls into the common good but does not give rise to a question as to the ability of the authority to alienate may seem small, in real terms it probably comprises the vast majority of common good properties – at least if the classification of common good property taken is that proposed by their Lordships in the *Ruthin Castle* case.

Land with no public use whatsoever

One case which is somewhat scanty authority for the view that land with no public use whatsoever may have no question as to alienability hanging over it, is *North East Fife District Council, Petitioners*[20]. This case concerned an area of land at Charles Street, Pittenweem, which was located near a pond in which a rare breed of newts lived. The objectors did not wish development as they did not want the newts to be disturbed. Accordingly, the court action

---

18 See **8.1**.
19 (1903) 6 F (HL) 10, (1903) 11 SLT 537.
20 Cupar Sh Ct, 1 March 1991, unreported.

was framed on the basis of withdrawal of amenities rather than any specific recreational purpose. The sheriff, somewhat reluctantly granting the petition of the district council, expressed a doubt as to whether the petition was necessary at all and held that there were no special attributes of the land such that it could be said to be inalienable. As already seen, in *East Lothian District Council v National Coal Board*, Lord Maxwell disapproved of the idea of refusing common good petitions as unnecessary[21].

Disposals on all fours with previous cases

The corollary of what has been said above about land which has already been the subject of previous case law is that if a proposed disposal turned on exactly the same sets of facts and circumstances as an alienation case which had been decided in favour of alienation, then it might be said that no question arises. However, it seems very unlikely that the facts and circumstances would ever be exactly the same – even if it were the same piece of land[22].

Land/buildings where the original purpose has disappeared

Where the original purpose of the land or buildings has disappeared is a slightly different set of circumstances from cases such as *Magistrates of Kirkcaldy v Marks & Spencer Ltd* or *Cockenzie and Port Seton Community Council v East Lothian District Council*. The circumstances in mind here would be something like a road which has been closed off under, for example, the Roads (Scotland) Act 1984, and which no longer serves a public purpose[23]. On one reading, the public purpose is now fulfilled by the alternative routes; on another reading, it could be said that the public purpose, at least so far as that road is concerned, has now disappeared. Another example might be if an area of ground had been used solely as a bleaching green in the past and for no other recreational purpose. In that

---

21 1982 SLT 460 at 469.

22 And see the facts and circumstances of *West Dunbartonshire Council v Harvie*, discussed at **8.4**.

23 Roads and streets in burghs which are still of use are generally inalienable: see *Young v Dobson* 2 Feb 1816 FC.

event, it would be difficult for the public to maintain that it was still required for that purpose given the technological changes to modern life. A third example might be an old slaughterhouse, given that, for various reasons, slaughterhouses are not now commonly featured in burghs. However, all of this would need to be approached with caution.

Land/buildings where public use has been interrupted for a substantial period

Clearly a question will still arise as to the authority's ability to alienate land or property in most cases. However, where a building has been used either by means of appropriation or alienation of some sort for a substantial period of time, it could be argued that no question arises as to the ability of the authority to alienate. However, the safest approach of all with this category would be to only assume that no question arises where the alienation or appropriation has taken place unchallenged for the long prescriptive period of twenty years, or at least no public use has taken place for that period. This approach might be over cautious for some properties which are clearly no longer *extra commercium*. Examples of this category might include industrial or retail concerns leased out to third parties and which are now proposed to be sold, either to the same parties, or to someone else.

In conclusion, the issue of when a question arises as to the ability of an authority to alienate is a vexed one. The safe approach is always to take the matter to court. However, there may be situations where it is so plainly a piece of property outwith public use that it is safe to proceed without reference to court.

The next chapter will consider the factors involved in allowing a disposal where the authority decides – or the community decides for them – that the case should proceed to court.

Chapter 8

Factors involved in allowing disposal

8.1 Pleading own neglect

Assuming an authority has decided that a question arises as to its ability to alienate a piece of ground, and it has decided either to alienate it or dispose of it, what are the factors involved in the court's decision to allow or disallow such disposal or alienation? The focus in this chapter will be principally on disposal simply because it is far more common in practice nowadays. There will then be a brief look at appropriations or alienations falling short of disposal in an attempt to determine some pointers as to how a court might deal with such matters nowadays.

So far as disposal under the 1973 Act is concerned, the approach taken by the courts so far is pragmatic, in that they weigh up what would be of most benefit to the community in the former burgh. However, before looking at the benefits, it is necessary to consider two cases which deal with the more fundamental point of why the property is being disposed of in the first place and whether, in fact, the authority's own neglect is the principal or main reason. If so, then a doctrine exists to the effect that an authority cannot plead its own neglect when seeking authorisation to dispose of common good property.

For many years, the main authority in this area was the nineteenth-century alienation case of *Grahame v Magistrates of Kirk-caldy*[1]. This case came up earlier, in **1.1**, as representing a classic example of the decline and fall of common good land after the

---

1 (1879) 6 R 1066. See also **6.4** for a discussion of this case in the context of "appropriation".

Industrial Revolution in the late eighteenth and nineteenth centuries. Briefly, the facts were that eight acres had been disponed by royal charter to the magistrates in 1644; in 1754 the land was disponed by the magistrates of the burgh to the then provost under reservation of a right to the inhabitants for drying linen cloths. When the property was disponed back in 1788, that burden remained. Between 1788 and 1804 all but about an acre had been feued off for building as the burgh expanded rapidly.

The remaining acre or so came to be known as the Volunteer's Green. The burgh ran a sewer through the middle of it and then a road. The north-most portion was kept open as a public bleaching green. The south-most part fell into disuse, mainly because the magistrates used it as a town dung stance. Although this use seems to have stopped after 1848, the ground was left in a pretty unsavoury state and its use for any sort of public recreation was very limited, although the case report notes that "some of the poorer class of people from the neighbouring houses occasionally laid out common articles of clothing to dry on a few patches of it where a little grass was left"[2].

When the magistrates disponed the ground to themselves as police commissioners and started to erect police stables on it, one of the residents had had enough. He raised an action of interdict against the burgh from building anything on the land.

The court, in coming to its decision, relied upon evidence led in a Kirkcaldy Sheriff Court case in 1854 between a Mr Heggie and the magistrates which described the state of the ground then and the public uses to which it had been put in the past. The Inner House, in adhering to the Lord Ordinary's decision to grant Mr Grahame's interdict, took the view that a dedication to public use could not be said to have ceased simply because the authority had, by its own neglect, caused it to cease. The Lord Justice-Clerk (Moncrieff) said:

> "But the Magistrates are not entitled to found upon their own negligence in the care of this piece of ground, for that is what it comes to, against the community which they represent. If this

2 At 1069.

ground was by grant or ancient use appropriated, or, as English lawyers would say, dedicated, to the purposes of recreation, drying clothes, and the like, the Magistrates were bound to see that it was kept in such order as to be suitable for these purposes. If it has been allowed to become unfit for these uses, that only shews that to that extent the duty of the Magistrates has been neglected . . . the possession of the ground as a drying-green has indeed been of late years much interrupted, and has in fact well nigh come to an end altogether, owing chiefly to the neglect of the Magistrates, to say nothing of their abuse of the ground by turning it into a public dung-stance. . . .

"Therefore, . . . on the whole matter, though I cannot doubt that the Corporation have acted in their judgment for the best interests of the community, I am of opinion that they were wrong in point of law, and that the community are entitled to vindicate their rights in this ground, however valueless these rights may be."[3]

This case does not appear to have been brought into play much in the reported case law so far. However, its implications are obvious for local authorities caught in possession of derelict land or buildings which they wish to dispose of. And although not actually following the *Grahame* case, the much more recent decision in *Stirling District Council, Petitioners*[4] should ring alarm bells for authorities with properties of this nature.

The case concerned the Museum Hall in Henderson Street, Bridge of Allan. Built in 1886–87, the property had something of a chequered history. Apart from requisition by the military during the First World War, it was owned and operated by a trust until 1938. In that year, the trust became insolvent and the hall was transferred to a limited company which ran it until 1950. It was then sold to the burgh council to be held "in all time coming for the benefit of the community of Bridge of Allan". The property had been offered to the burgh when the trust went insolvent in 1938, but it had refused to take it on. One of the reasons it had

3 At 1073.
4 Outer House, 19 May 2000, unreported: available on www.scotcourts. gov.uk.

done so was that there were structural problems inherent in the site from its original construction.

However, Lord Penrose also found from the evidence provided by the court-appointed reporter that there was "eloquent evidence of a consistent failure to maintain the building during the steward-ship of the local authorities following public acquisition in 1950". Lord Penrose went on:

> "Had these elements of deterioration told the whole story, one would have hesitated to conclude that the petitioners, who in large parts have succeeded to the consequences of the neglect of their predecessors, should be relieved of the obligation to maintain this listed building."

However, given the very costly and complicated engineering exercise required to bring the building back into beneficial use, Lord Penrose said:

> "I am satisfied that it would be unreasonable to refuse the prayer of the petition on the ground that its state was the responsibility of the petitioners, and to leave the petitioners exposed to the obli-gations relating to the structure which would follow from their ownership of a listed building which had to be restored for public use."

It seems clear from this judgment that Lord Penrose had it in mind that, if the neglect of the building had been solely due to the local authority, then he would not have authorised its disposal. Authorities with similar buildings or areas of land should take note of this point when considering the next case.

8.2   Prioritisation of limited funding

The above two cases on neglect can be contrasted, to some extent, with the approach taken by Lord Kirkwood in *Motherwell District Council, Petitioners*[5]. The subject-matter in this case was a park of 7.89 acres in Wishaw which had been donated in 1921 to the then

---

5 1988 GWD 15-666 (OH).

local authority under a title provision that the grounds should, in all time coming, be kept in good condition as a public park for the use and enjoyment of the whole community of the burgh of Motherwell and Wishaw. Although, initially, this was the case, the park had deteriorated and, by the time of the petition, was described as being "virtually derelict".

The district council's proposals for the park consisted of disposing of 1.9 acres of it to Strathclyde Regional Council for a replacement primary school, with the playing surface at the primary school being available for public use outwith school hours; a purchase price of £50,000; and realignment of a servitude right of access to the owners of an adjoining coach works. Another acre was proposed to be leased under a 125-year lease to developers of a retail food store which was to be erected on the former coach works site. The one acre part of the park would be used for car parking for the food store. A lease premium to be paid by the developer would be in the region of £240,000.

The park would accordingly reduce from 7.9 acres to around 5 acres which would be the subject of a comprehensive improvement scheme by the council including provision of an all-weather, full-sized playing surface, security fencing, floodlighting and a brick-clad sports pavilion as well as substantial areas for landscaping, walking, recreation and informal play.

Central Wishaw Community Council, who opposed the application, argued that the present state of the park was due to years of neglect by the district council and its predecessors which it could not now found on in support of the application. Motherwell District Council, they argued, should have explored the possibility of marketing land for some other type of development with a view to bringing in the maximum money for the minimum land. Clearly, this approach followed the line taken in cases such as *Grahame*.

Lord Kirkwood, however, disagreed. Perhaps surprisingly, he took the view that the district council had, over the years, prioritised its limited funding and that it was entitled to do so. There was a need for modern sporting and recreational facilities of the standard proposed by Motherwell and implementation of the proposals would be in the long-term interests of the local community.

Commenting on the funding, he noted that the development proposals currently in hand were at least available now and it would not be sensible to require Motherwell to begin to search for other possible types of development which might be fruitless and lead to the loss of the two sources now available.

It is a little difficult to reconcile this approach with some of the judicial comments made in both the *Grahame* and *Stirling District Council* cases discussed at **8.1** above. In particular, Lord Penrose in the *Stirling* case seemed keen to apportion blame. He seems to have been inclined, had the fault of the building's current state been solely that of the local authority and its predecessor authorities, to refuse the prayer of the petition. Lord Kirkwood in the *Motherwell District Council* case seems to have been less concerned with apportioning blame and more concerned with establishing what would be in the best interests of the community.

This approach can also be contrasted with the earlier *Grahame* case, where the Lord Justice-Clerk commented that "the community are entitled to vindicate their rights in this ground, however valueless those rights may be"[6]. That case was, of course, decided long before the advent of the current statutory provisions and it seems that the courts now consider different considerations apply.

8.3   Balance of convenience to the burgh residents

A similar approach to that of Lord Kirkwood in *Motherwell District Council* was taken by Lord Caplan in *Kirkcaldy District Council v Burntisland Community Council*[7]. This case concerned a public caravan park, part of a larger estate of land bought by the burgh of Burntisland in 1907 under a common good wording. Although that wording did not extend to any specific purpose, the council minutes recorded that the proposal to buy the land was "to acquire lands in the neighbourhood suitable for recreation grounds and other municipal purposes".

The ground had been used for various public purposes over the

6 (1879) 6 R at 1073.
7 1993 SLT 753.

years. It had been a refuse disposal site until around 1954. Adjoining land was originally used as a football pitch. Other small parts of the land were used for grazing, allotments and other miscellaneous purposes. In 1954, all the land was converted to use as a caravan site. Used for static caravans by principally West of Scotland caravan owners, the site was a loss-making enterprise primarily because an amenity block on the caravan site, paid for out of the leisure and recreation capital account, created borrowings which had to be repaid out of an ever diminishing income from the caravanners.

The district council sought to get authority from the court to dispose of the land to British Alcan, then the largest employer in Burntisland. A reporter was appointed and he found that, if the land was not sold to British Alcan, there was a very real danger that it would have to take its expansion plans elsewhere and this would be a major blow to the local economy.

Lord Caplan commented that the community seemed to be receiving an economic benefit from the land rather than a recreational benefit and that this could be better served by the proposals to transfer the land to British Alcan, as those proposals would create a much better economic benefit. Although not all of the land which comprised the caravan site was presently needed by the local employer, it was likely that its expansion plans would continue in the future and that, therefore, all of the land should be authorised for disposal now to save the expense of a further petition to the court.

To an extent, therefore, the case had a peculiar set of facts. Although all parties conceded that a question arose as to the ability of the authority to alienate, the "recreational purpose" of the land was not a recreational purpose so far as the residents of the burgh were concerned – except to the extent that any of them wanted to go on holiday in their home town. The recreational purpose was enjoyed by people from elsewhere in the country. On the other hand, there was a clear economic benefit to the people of Burntisland in authorising the disposal of the land. Lord Caplan said:

> "Clearly, in order to discharge its powers, the court requires to pay attention to the nature and quality of the rights which the inhabi-

tants of the locality enjoy over the land under consideration. Any inhabitants who enjoy a specific exercisable right over the land should not be readily disadvantaged. In this regard, however, it should again be noted that it is not at all certain that any inhabitants of Burntisland have, in fact, personally used the said land for many years."[8]

Commenting on the judgment call that had to be made on continuation of the caravan park or sale to the company, Lord Caplan said:

> The petitioners, as the local authority charged with certain responsibility regarding the economic welfare of the community, are well placed to make that judgment. Accordingly, their view is entitled to some respect and on the facts it is one with which I have no difficulty in agreeing."[9]

One minor point of interest in this case which might reappear in future was that, because of the peculiarities of the transaction, a value above that assessed by the district valuer had been negotiated with the proposed purchasers. The petitioner sought to have this extra amount applied towards the loans for construction of the amenity block. Lord Caplan refused this and directed that the whole proceeds should be transferred to the common good account, commenting that expenditure on the amenity block

> "was not regarded as a charge on the relevant common good fund, so that the position in law appears to be that the petitioners have chosen to amplify the value of the land (and thus the common good fund which it represents) by erecting a building on it. . . . If the petitioners translate the fund into money by selling the land, the proceeds remain subject to the common good trust."[10]

It is clear, therefore, that where there is an obvious benefit to the community, then the court is likely to be minded to authorise disposal subject, of course, to the financial benefit being translated into the common good fund of the area. However, authorities have not

8 At 757.
9 At 758.
10 At 758.

had it all their own way in relation to disposals of this kind, as will be seen with the next case.

8.4   No clear benefit

The case of *West Dunbartonshire Council v Harvie*[11] concerned an area of ground in the centre of Dumbarton known as Dumbarton Common. It extended to around 12.84 acres. It had been used for public recreation for many centuries in the case of part of it and from the middle of the nineteenth century in respect of the remainder which had been reclaimed from the sea. A sports centre was built on the common as well as a children's playground. A public footpath crossed it. In 1990 the Court of Session had granted permission to Dumbarton District Council to grant a lease for ninety-nine years for what was described as a public indoor bowling stadium. However, that project never proceeded.

In 1995, Dumbarton District Council entered into missives with the Secretary of State for Scotland for the erection of a new building on the same area as the abortive bowling stadium project. The proposal was for a new sheriff courthouse. This was a replacement for a listed building elsewhere in Dumbarton which was no longer fit for purpose. The site, which was the subject of the petition, extended to 1.44 acres out of the total 12.84 acres, and was seen as a suitable site for a replacement by the council and the Secretary of State.

As is common in Court of Session common good cases, a reporter was appointed to investigate the facts to avoid the expense of a lengthy proof. The reporter found that all parties were agreed that the sheriff court should stay in Dumbarton, for historical and economic reasons, but that there was considerable dispute on what was the best site. It is fair to say that the petitioners relied heavily on the Scottish Courts Service's preference for the Dumbarton Common site and this seemed to prove their undoing in the Outer House before Lord MacLean. He said:

---

11 1997 SLT 979 (OH); 1998 SC 789, 1998 SCLR 639 (Ex Div).

"Unless the petitioners make abundantly clear all the considerations which persuaded the Secretary of State to prefer the
Dumbarton Common site above all others, it makes the task of the
court very difficult when it comes to weigh all the competing considerations in the balance. I do not think it is sufficient for the petitioners merely to state the Secretary of State's preference. One
would have to know whether, for example, the Church Street site
[an alternative site where the existing sheriff court building was
located] could be developed physically, using the present building
or buildings. If it could, what is the anticipated cost of that? Is that
cost considered beyond the means of government? How does that
cost compare with the cost of erecting a new building on the
Dumbarton common? Is there a locational advantage of one site
over the other? Are there traffic and parking considerations? I
merely throw up these questions at random. But the fact that the
petitioners have not made available any such information lend
some support for the submission . . . that the petitioners should
have satisfied themselves that the Scottish Courts Service's preference was based on grounds which were sufficient to outweigh any
presumption in favour of retaining common good land or to outweigh any presumption in favour of retaining open ground."[12]

Lord MacLean also commented on the fact that the Secretary
of State, the purchaser of the land, had not been served with the
petition. This, it seemed to him, was unfortunate in that he was not
able to ascertain the Secretary of State's position directly by means
of answers.

Because of the perceived lack of information before him, Lord
MacLean was not convinced that there would be any clear benefit
in locating the sheriff court at that particular site. Although there
was a general acceptance that, if the sheriff court was not situated in
Dumbarton, there would be some economic loss in terms of jobs
and spending power and also some indefinable loss in terms of "the
sense of community", that was, in the end, an argument for
locating the new sheriff court somewhere in Dumbarton and not
necessarily on that particular site.

Nor was Lord MacLean convinced that the interference with

12 At 981–982.

existing recreation proposed by the petitioners was of a minor nature. All the existing facilities could be relocated or realigned. However, the inhabitants who opposed the petition, and who appeared as party litigants, made a convincing case for the land being part of the only public park in Dumbarton town centre, and as being a "green lung" for the centre of town. Lord MacLean said:

> "In my opinion, such public open space, used freely for recreational purposes, is a vital amenity for all inhabitants of towns and cities. In this case it is an amenity which has been enjoyed for centuries. Why should that amenity not be enjoyed for several hundred more years? It would, in my opinion, take a very compelling case to justify an encroachment on the land for the erection of a public building which did not fulfil the recreational purposes for which the land had so long been used. I do not consider the petitioners have properly weighed the *actual* and permanent loss of such common good land against the *potential* loss of a new Sheriff Court building in Dumbarton."[13]

On appeal, the Extra Division of the Inner House was reluctant to interfere with the Lord Ordinary's decision. The Lord Ordinary, it said, was entitled to have regard to matters which, in his view, the petitioners had failed to establish as well as to those matters on which they had satisfied him. It was not for the court to make investigations into the benefits or disbenefits of the proposal, but to consider the information put before it, such as it was. Accordingly, the Lord Ordinary had not misdirected himself.

There are clearly lessons to be learned for local authorities and potential objectors to proposed disposals out of the common good from this case. Clearly, any potential purchaser of such land should be brought into the action as a respondent so that answers can, if the court so desires, be lodged and an appearance made to clarify the position in a case of this nature. One wonders, however, whether appearance by the Secretary of State in this particular case would have made that much difference. Clearly, the Scottish Courts Service preferred the prospect of a greenfield site rather than

13 At 983.

working on a restricted site incorporating a listed building with all the design and financial implications that would have had. Lord MacLean seemed not to consider that enough of a justification in itself.

Similarly, the existence of a sheriff courthouse taking land away from a recreational area used by the residents of the burgh was a much less clear-cut benefit than the Burntisland case discussed in **8.3** above, where the choice was between expansion of a major employer and the loss of a recreational purpose which was making a loss and did not directly benefit the residents of the burgh anyway.

For any potential objector, however, the decision must offer some encouragement. The three respondents appeared as party litigants before Lord MacLean and, despite the best efforts of one of the then senior members of the bar (who was commended by Lord MacLean for his assistance to the court), they carried the day.

The reality is that there is not very much to choose between the facts and circumstances surrounding the three cases of *Motherwell District Council, Petitioners, Kirkcaldy District Council v Burntisland Community Council* and *West Dunbartonshire Council v Harvie*. All concerned inalienable common good land which was being used for rough and ready recreational provision of one kind or another. In each case, the proposed use would bring benefits of one kind or another. Clearly, however, each case will be looked at by the courts on its own merits and, perhaps, on the quality of the evidence led on any supposed benefits as well as the potential loss to the community.

8.5   Alienations and appropriations

This leaves the modern-day cases which fall out of the ambit of disposals for the purposes of the 1973 Act, as discussed in chapter 7. In such cases, it would appear that the choices for the local authority in seeking to get court approval are rather more stark. It cannot petition the court under section 75(2) for authority to alienate or appropriate the land if such alienation or appropriation falls short of disposal.

It would appear that the local authority can seek a declarator that the land in question does not form part of the inalienable common good but that it has, for some reason, either always been capable of alienation, or has become so, perhaps by means of re-placement premises now being available; or, perhaps, that section 20 of the Local Government in Scotland Act 2003 applies in that the proposed alienation or appropriation advances the well-being of the area or its people[14].

The next chapter deals with the practicalities of taking a common good case to court.

14 See **2.3** and **6.4**.

Chapter 9

Taking a common good case to court

9.1 Forms of action

Section 75 of the Local Government (Scotland) Act 1973 allows local authorities to take petitions for disposal of land forming part of the common good either to the Court of Session or the sheriff court.

So far as the Court of Session is concerned, the provisions governing petitions can be found in Chapter 14 of the Rules of Court. Normally, such petitions would be dealt with, in the first instance, in the Outer House[1]. In the majority of modern cases concerning disposal which have come before the Court of Session, the court has either *ex proprio motu*, or at the instance of the parties, appointed a reporter to investigate the facts and revert to the court with a report setting out the factual position. The reporter is normally an advocate of some standing who has experience in matters of this kind. The advantage of this procedure is that it cuts down on the amount of court time, and therefore expense, taken up with hearing facts which are clearly not in dispute.

Finally on the Court of Session, rule 34 provides for a report by the Lord Ordinary to the Inner House for a ruling on any matter

---

1 Act of Sederunt (Rules of the Court of Session 1994) 1994 (SI 1994/ 1443), rule 14.2(h) would appear to apply. For both Court of Session and Sheriff Court Rules of Court, a handy resource is www.scotcourts.gov.uk. In *East Lothian District Council v National Coal Board* 1982 SLT 460, the report mentions that the Inner House had directed that in future all common good petitions would be heard by the Inner House. However, that practice does not seem to have been followed since.

of particular complexity. This is what happened in the recent *South Lanarkshire Council* case[2] where the case was put out for a hearing before a Division of the Inner House on the summar roll.

In the sheriff court, such guidance as there is can be found in the current Sheriff Court Ordinary Cause Rules[3]. The general practice in sheriff court actions does not appear to be to appoint a reporter. Where the action is defended, it is more likely that a hearing will be fixed on evidential matters.

A style petition to the sheriff court has been reproduced, with some trepidation, as Appendix II. This is purely for guidance only. The important point to note is that the sheriff, even if he or she is familiar with this area of law and the property to be disposed of, is likely to require considerable evidential support for the council's position, and this will require to be set up in the condescendence.

There is nothing in the 1973 Act or elsewhere to guide a local authority as to whether it should take the case to the sheriff court or the Court of Session. On the one hand, having the case heard locally before a sheriff who might have knowledge of the area may have some advantages. The most obvious advantage is a saving on cost for all concerned. In addition, the hearing of the case locally will be more convenient for all parties and, in particular, those community groups and representatives who might wish to oppose the petition will be more able to attend court and have their say. This is surely desirable even for the local authority if it wishes to be seen to be a "listening authority".

On the other hand, there are clear disadvantages in taking the matter to a sheriff court. Common good applications, although becoming more and more frequent, are still relatively infrequent on an individual sheriff court basis. It may be that there is not a great amount of expertise in the sheriff court area – either amongst solicitors representing the parties or the sheriffs – to deal with a particularly complex common good case. Such expertise as exists generally lies in the hands of Court of Session judges and a select number of advocates. There is nothing, of course, to stop either the

---

2 Inner House, 11 August 2004, unreported.
3 Act of Sederunt (Sheriff Court Ordinary Cause Rules) 1993 (SI 1993/ 1956) also available on www.scotcourts.gov.uk.

local authority or objectors from engaging counsel in a sheriff court application. However, that would seem to be an uncomfortable half-way house between a "run of the mill" sheriff court action and an action in the Court of Session itself.

The Court of Session has the advantages described, and perhaps one other main plus point. If the case is particularly complex, it is more likely that precedent can be followed or distinguished more easily.

The main disadvantages of a Court of Session action are time, expense (subject to what will be said shortly on award of expenses) and inconvenience to the parties. It would certainly not seem to be an appropriate way of dealing with a common good application which is likely to be unopposed because the community is in agreement with it.

A case regarding common good may, of course, appear in court by means of a procedure other than a section 75 petition. If there is doubt as to whether what is proposed amounts to a "disposal" under section 75 of the 1973 Act, then the authority may wish to couple the petition with an action of declarator that the land or building in question does not form part of the inalienable part of the common good. However, this is likely to be procedurally difficult.

The likely forms of action available to objectors have been already touched upon briefly in earlier chapters. An action of interdict, for example, was used in the case of *Waddell v Stewartry District Council*[4]. However, an application for interdict – especially if coupled with a crave for interim interdict – raises its own perils for the person taking such action in terms of expenses.

An earlier chapter[5] discussed the possibility of judicial review. As outlined in *Cockenzie and Port Seton Community Council v East Lothian District Council*[6], the court is unlikely to hold that disposal of common good property is either unreasonable in the *Wednesbury* sense or *ultra vires* in the sense that the council has no statutory power to do so – even if no section 75 petition has been raised.

4 1977 SLT (Notes) 35.
5 See **3.1**.
6 1997 SLT 81.

The only other remedy which seems apparently available to objectors is that of action of reduction of a disposition – or challenge to the Keeper's issue of a land certificate – where a local authority has disposed of a common good property without reference to the court. It would clearly be unfortunate if matters went as far as that without the issue having been taken to court by means of a section 75 petition. Indeed, there is some tentative authority in *Grahame v Magistrates of Kirkcaldy*[7] for the proposition that disposition to a third party might not be capable of challenge in this way. In that case, of course, the disposition was between the magistrates and the magistrates acting as police commissioners – hardly an arm's length transaction. However, Lord Ormidale commented:

> "The result might be different if a stranger, in ignorance of the true rights of the inhabitants, had, in good faith, acquired title to some part of the common good in question from the respondents. Such an acquisition might perhaps be unchallengeable."[8]

If matters were to proceed along that line, it would appear that a local authority could still, by way of a defence, seek authority of the court under section 75(2), as there is nothing specifically in the wording that suggests that the authority of the court requires to be obtained before disposal – although that is clearly what is intended and should normally be the practice.

What emerges from the case law is a clear indication that other forms of action are all rather difficult and it would clearly be preferable in every case where there is likely to be litigation over the proposal that the local authority takes the lead and presents the section 75 petition to court – unless, of course, the case concerns an alienation falling short of a section 75 disposal.

9.2   Advertisement

In all actions, under section 75, it is likely that the local authority will be expected to advertise the application in a local newspaper.

7 (1879) 6 R 1066.
8 At 1075–1076.

This is a course of action to be recommended as it will give the community one last chance to mount any formal opposition. There is no statutory formula for advertisement and there are appended, again as a very rough style, forms which have been used successfully in the past[9].

At the same time as this advertisement is inserted, consideration should be given to whether advertisement is required under other statutes, such as the disposal of open space provisions under the Town and Country Planning (Scotland) Act 1959[10], or regulations to be made under section 74 of the Local Government (Scotland) Act 1973 (as inserted by section 11 of the Local Government in Scotland Act 2003)[11].

9.3 Consultation

In most instances, local authorities will have clearly defined consultation protocols with community councils and these should be followed in the case of disposals of common good land, even where it is thought that the proposal is uncontroversial or that no question arises. The fact that there was no such consultation is unlikely to make the authority susceptible to successful judicial review[12]. However, such consultation would seem to be prudent as a court, in considering a section 75 application, is likely to wish to have it demonstrated that all the issues have been fully explored and the options weighed up properly.

In the consultation process, the local authority should also consult with other community groups. Clearly, in a contentious issue like the disposal of common good land, it is unlikely that a consensus can ever be reached and the best that a local authority can hope for is to show that it has had regard to all issues raised by the com-

9 See Appendix III.
10 Section 27, as amended by Local Government (Miscellaneous Provisions) (Scotland) Act 1981, s 25, Sch 2, para 10. On appropriations, see s 24 of the 1959 Act and Sch 2, para 9.
11 See **2.2**.
12 See, for a non-common good example, R *(City of Westminster) v Mayor of London* [2002] EWHC 2240.

munity in one form or another and taken all relevant matters into account in coming to its decision to proceed.

West Dunbartonshire Council v Harvie is authority for the proposition that there was no obligation on the local authority to consult the community in any particular way. Lord MacLean said:

> "Had there been little or no consultation within the community that would have been a factor which I would have had to take into account. But where there has been general consultation and an informed decision has been taken by the elected members of the local authority, that factor loses much of the weight it might otherwise have had."[13]

9.4   Expenses

The rule of thumb in most court actions is, of course, that expenses follow success. However, the matter is not quite so clear-cut in court actions relating to the common good. In *Fife Council v Leven Community Council*[14], Sheriff Keane awarded expenses in favour of the community council. In doing so, he referred to the case of *Crawford v Magistrates of Paisley*[15]. The only reason that case had proceeded to the Inner House was in relation to the award of expenses and, because Mr Crawford had been justified in the particular procedure he had taken in the Court of Session, the main part of the expenses was awarded in his favour. However, there does not, from the survey results reproduced at Appendix V, seem to be any particular practice adopted on award of expenses.

A more difficult question is whether those expenses should be met from the common good fund. In some cases, such as *Kirkcaldy District Council v Burntisland Community Council*[16], the disposal proceeds are directed to be paid into the common good less the expenses of disposal. Local authorities might legitimately argue that the expenses of the court action would constitute part of the

13   1997 SLT 979 at 982.
14   Kirkcaldy Sh Ct, 25 July 2001, unreported.
15   (1870) 8 M 693.
16   1993 SLT 753.

expenses of disposal and that, therefore, they should be met from the sale proceeds.

So much for common good in the courts. The final chapter looks at common good in the twenty-first century.

Chapter 10

Common good in the twenty-first century

10.1 Unanswered questions

To say that common good has become a controversial topic is to give the wrong impression. The truth is that it has always been controversial. From the earliest reported cases, such as *Fram v Magistrates of Dumbarton*[1], a case concerning the rights of burgesses to have salmon caught from the burgh lands sold to them at a discount price, to more recent cases such as *South Lanarkshire Council, Petitioners*[2] on such matters as PPP schools being built on recreational land, little has changed. The structure of an authority might be different nowadays but the inhabitants of the burghs have always seen it as their duty to defend their charter privileges as vigorously as the law allows[3].

This centuries-old conflict between the "magistrates" and the inhabitants has, as indicated in the preface, produced a law on common good which is largely based on sound, sensible, well-reasoned principles arising from case law. Chapter 2 showed that a statutory framework of sorts exists but it is, to a very great extent, supplemented by the common law and has itself been subject to considerable judicial interpretation, particularly in relation to land disposal under section 75 of the Local Government (Scotland) Act 1973.

However, some questions remain. The first of these is in relation to those cases concerning land over which the public have acquired

1 (1786) Mor 2002.
2 Inner House, 11 August 2004, unreported.
3 And indeed, beyond, in some cases: see *Dempster v Cleghorn (case of St Andrews)* (1805) Mor 16141, rem (1813) 2 Dow 40.

rights such as recreation. Is it sufficient for this possession to have been for the prescriptive period? Or is there, as is indicated in the case law, a requirement that the title itself be "ancient"[4]?

Another question which has never been resolved directly, although there is considerable judicial commentary on it, is that of disposals which are not challenged at the time. Does the new owner have to wait out the long negative prescriptive period to ensure the rights of the inhabitants cannot be vindicated against him, as is suggested in *Paterson v Magistrates of St Andrews*[5]? Would acquisition in good faith by a genuine third party be unchallengeable as is suggested in *Grahame v Magistrates of Kirkcaldy*[6]? The judicial commentary on this point is largely obiter.

A third unresolved question relates to **1.4** and the discussion in it on common good and trusts. Whilst the reported cases such as *Magistrates of Banff v Ruthin Castle Ltd*[7] and *Wilson v Inverclyde Council*[8] give some guidance on the matter, there remains a doubt as to whether a public trust could ever be created by way of a disposition of heritable property with more specific wording.

Fourthly, the whole issue of how common good fund monies can be applied by local authorities has yet to be tested. As outlined in **3.3**, there seems to be an inherent tension between a local authority's statutory obligation to obtain overall best value for all of its assets and performance and the requirement that, in administering the common good, a local authority must have regard to the interests of (with the exception of the four largest cities) only a small part of its overall area – the former burgh.

Perhaps these questions can be answered only by future case law.

10.2   Common good and partnerships

If there is one area where the use of common good property is

---

4 See **4.3**.
5 (1880) 7 R 712, (1881) 8 R (HL) 117.
6 (1879) 6 R 1066.
7 1944 SC 36, 1944 SLT 373.
8 2003 SC 366, 2004 SLT 265.

likely to raise questions that require judicial determination, it is that of disposal, or alienation, of such property in a partnership setting.

Partnership working is one of the central aims of modern governmental policy. At a national and local level, corporate bodies that have, in the past, operated independently of, or even on occasion in opposition to, each other are now being urged to work together for the public good. As between public organisations, this desire is now enshrined in the provisions of the Local Government in Scotland Act 2003 relating to community planning. At every level, local government is also being asked to work with the private sector to produce a better result. Funding sources previously given to local government are now only available through such partnership bodies as can be created.

The net effect of this is that common good land and buildings – and, potentially, common good funds – are likely to be used increasingly in new ways. Inevitably this will focus principally on the disposal of common good land and buildings to assist some partnership objective – whether it be a PPP school, delivery of a health facility as part of a Joint Futures project, or even disposal to a community group for a specified purpose which is seen to be desirable.

Laudable as many of these projects may be, all of them will fall foul of the alienation prohibition on some common good land. Again, future case law may make it clear whether the sometimes complex partnership arrangements entered into by local authorities these days on such matters as PPP projects constitute a disposal under the 1973 Act, or whether they amount to alienations or appropriations falling short of disposal.

10.3   Proposals for reform

In a book designed to explain the law of common good, it is not really the writer's business to make proposals for reform. That is a matter for politicians and legislators. However, perhaps the following suggestions as to how the law might change could be seen as a starting-point for future debate.

It was said in the preface that the common good could be seen as little more than a historical appendix. Certainly, it might seem that way to inhabitants of towns nearby to former burghs which, through sheer historical accident, had never been elevated to burgh status. The existence of a separate fund – in some cases quite considerable – within the local authority coffers to be spent in such a way as has regard to the interests of the former burgh's residents, might seem a little inequitable to the former burgh's neighbours.

On the other hand, it may be that the former burgh's residents would claim that local authority mainstream funding has been diverted elsewhere as a result of the existence of the common good fund. They may have a point. But whatever the rights and wrongs of the issue, it is clear, given that the common good has survived more than two local government reorganisations and the abolition of the feudal system, it is not likely to disappear overnight.

Several options exist for reform if there is ever a political will to undertake it. One of the most simple reforms would be to abolish the distinction between the common good and the general fund of local authorities and do away with the common law rules relating to alienation of common good property by specific statutory provision. Such a solution would certainly have the benefit of simplicity. However, it is unlikely to gain favour in the former burghs.

The opposite solution to that would be to transfer the management and ownership of the common good to community councils or to some other community body where such exists in the former burghs. Whilst this solution might seem attractive to many burgh residents, distrustful of the motives of large, distant local authorities, it would have a number of obvious disadvantages.

For a start, it would make no sense in the four larger cities where the boundaries of the common good are contiguous with those of the local authority. In the smaller former burghs, questions of capacity might arise. Community council members are volunteers who are not paid for their service to the community. Many of them have full-time jobs. If community bodies were to take on the common good fund and its assets, the net effect might be to increase expenditure out of the common good on professional advisers and consultants required to ensure the fund and its assets were properly administered.

A middle way might be to abolish the distinction between the common good and general funds of local authorities but to impose extra obligations on local authorities for properties that have historic or recreational significance – whether or not these exist within former burghs. In many instances, the principal concern of communities has been the disappearance of recreational land, or the unsympathetic conversion of historic property of one kind or another by local authorities who, in some instances, have neglected the properties for years. Perhaps if that is the main issue, then it should be recognised as such. Local authorities could be tasked with keeping a register of such properties; they could also be required to allow disposal only if specific criteria can be met and if no community use can be reasonably found after diligent investigation.

However, such issues as these are, as stated already, for legislators and politicians and not for the lawyers amongst us who do not fall into either category. What is clear is that, unless the concept of common good is swept away by legislation, it will remain the focus of debate within the walls of the court and the council chamber for some time to come[9].

---

9 For a recent exploration of the issues rehearsed briefly in this chapter, see Andy Wightman and James Perman, *Common Good Land in Scotland. A Review & Critique* (2005) available via www.caledonia.org.uk.

Appendix I

List of burghs[1]

Aberdeen	Dundee	Edinburgh	Glasgow

LARGE BURGHS

Airdrie	Dunfermline	Motherwell and Wishaw
Arbroath	Falkirk	Paisley
Ayr	Greenock	Perth
Clydebank	Hamilton	Port Glasgow
Coatbridge	Inverness	Rutherglen
Dumbarton	Kilmarnock	Stirling
Dumfries	Kirkcaldy	

SMALL BURGHS

Aberchirder	Dalkeith	Kilwinning
Aberfeldy	Darvel	Kinghorn
Aberlour	Denny and Dunipace	Kingussie
Abernethy	Dingwall	Kinross
Alloa	Dollar	Kintore
Alva	Dornoch	Kirkcudbright
Alyth	Doune	Kirkintilloch
Annan	Dufftown	Kirkwall
Ardrossan	Dunbar	Kirriemuir
Armadale	Dunblane	Ladybank
Auchterarder	Dunoon	Lanark
Auchtermuchty	Duns	Langholm
Ballater	East Linton	Largs
Banchory	Elgin	Lauder
Banff	Elie and Earlsferry	Laurencekirk
Barrhead	Ellon	Lerwick
Bathgate	Eyemouth	Leslie
Biggar	Falkland	Leven

1 As set out in the First Schedule to the Local Government (Scotland) Act 1947. Nb the First Schedule set out "counties of cities", large burghs and small burghs. See **2.2**.

Blairgowrie and
  Rattray
Bo'ness
Bonnyrigg and
  Lasswade
Brechin
Bridge of Allan
Buckhaven and
  Methil
Buckie
Burghead
Burntisland
Callander
Campbeltown
Carnoustie
Castle Douglas
Cockenzie and Port
  Seton
Coldstream
Coupar Angus
Cove and Kilcreggan
Cowdenbeath
Crail
Crieff
Cromarty
Cullen
Culross
Cumnock and
  Holmhead
Cupar
Dalbeattie
Pittenweem
Portknockie
Portsoy
Prestonpans
Prestwick
Queensferry
Renfrew
Rosehearty
Rothes
Rothesay
St Andrews

Findochty
Forfar
Forres
Fortrose
Fort William
Fraserburgh
Galashiels
Galston
Gatehouse
Girvan
Gourock
Grangemouth
Grantown-on-Spey
Haddington
Helensburgh
Huntly
Innerleithen
Inveraray
Inverbervie
Invergordon
Inverkeithing
Inverurie
Irvine
Jedburgh
Johnstone
Keith
Kelso
Kilrenny, Anstruther
  Easter and Anstruther
  Wester
Kilsyth
St Monance
Saltcoats
Sanquhar
Selkirk
Stewarton
Stonehaven
Stornoway
Stranraer
Stromness
Tain
Tayport

Linlithgow
Loanhead
Lochgelly
Lochgilphead
Lochmaben
Lockerbie
Lossiemouth and
  Branderburgh
Macduff
Markinch
Maybole
Melrose
Millport
Milngavie
Monifeith
Montrose
Musselburgh
Nairn
Newburgh
New Galloway
Newmilns and
  Greenholm
Newport
Newton-Stewart
North Berwick
Oban
Oldmeldrum
Peebles
Penicuik
Peterhead
Pitlochry
Thurso
Tillicoultry
Tobermory
Tranent
Troon
Turriff
Whitburn
Whithorn
Wick
Wigtown

Appendix II

Style writ

SHERIFFDOM OF UTOPIA AT DEENBURGH

SUMMARY APPLICATION

under Section 75(2) of the Local Government (Scotland) Act 1973

Petition

by

THE UTOPIA COUNCIL constituted under the Local Government etc (Scotland) Act 1994 and having their principal offices at Utopia House, North Street, Deenburgh

PETITIONERS

under Section 75(2) of the Local Government (Scotland) Act 1973

for

Authority to dispose of land forming part of the Common Good land at Deenburgh under Section 75(2) of the Local Government (Scotland) Act 1973

The Petitioners hereby respectfully crave and Petition the Court;

1. To authorise the Petitioners to dispose of that mansion house and associated piece of land known as and forming Toff House,

Deenburgh shown outlined red on the plan produced with this Petition (Number 1 of Process), (hereinafter referred to as "the Subjects").

2. To appoint this application to be intimated upon Deenburgh Community Council, Toff House Action, the Gertrude Hyde Preservation Society[1], and to be advertised in the East Utopia Mail[2].

CONDESCENDENCE

1. The Petitioners are the Local Authority for Utopia in terms of the Local Government etc (Scotland) Act 1994. They are proprietors of the subject matter of this Petition as statutory successors to the former Burgh of Deenburgh in terms of Section 222 of the Local Government (Scotland) Act 1973; the Local Authorities (Property etc) Order 1975 (Article 4); the Local Government etc (Scotland) Act 1994 (section 15); and the Local Authorities (Property Transfer) (Scotland) Order 1995 (article 2). To the knowledge of the Petitioners there are no other proceedings pending before any other Court involving the present cause of action and between the parties hereto. To the knowledge of the Petitioners no agreement exists between the parties prorogating jurisdiction over the subject matter of the present cause to another Court. The land to which the Petition is addressed is situated in the former Burgh of Deenburgh. This Court accordingly has jurisdiction.

2. In 1856 the Trustees of Sir John Barleycorn disponed the Subjects to the Provost, Magistrates and Councillors of the Burgh of Deenburgh.

3. The Disposition narrated that Sir John Barleycorn had intimated a wish, acted upon by his trustees by means of the Dispo-

---

1 All interested parties the local authority is aware of should be served with a copy of the writ.
2 A local paper circulating in the area should be used for the advertisement: see Appendix III.

sition, to hand over the Subjects to the Provost, Magistrates and Councillors for the Burgh of Deenburgh:

"As a gift to be used for the benefit of the community of Deenburgh."[3]

The Disposition is dated Twenty-ninth August and subsequent dates and recorded in the Division of the General Register of Sasines for the County of Utopia on Fifteenth September all dates in the year 1856. A copy of said Disposition is lodged in process (Number 2 of Process) and held to be incorporated herein brevitatis causa.

4. After its acquisition, Toff House, which forms part of the Subjects, was initially used for the general administration of the Burgh. After the erection of new municipal buildings in or around 1902, the building was used as a temporary fever hospital until its requisitioning by the Crown for barracks during the First World War. On its return to the management of the Burgh in 1919, it was used as a Central Kitchen until 1939, when it was again requisitioned by the Crown. From 1949 onwards it was used for the accommodation of staff engaged in various departments of the former Burgh, but principally in connection with leisure and recreation. After local government reorganisation in 1975, and again in 1996, the building housed leisure and recreation staff until its closure in 2004 as a result of rationalisation of Utopia Council's Leisure Services Division.

5. The remainder of the Subjects originally formed part of the policies of Toff House, and had been laid out in a design created by the landscape gardener Gertrude Hyde. During its occupation as a fever hospital a tennis court was built in the south east corner for convalescents. During its occupation by the Army in 1914–19 the original gardens were obliterated and the grounds used as a test firing range. Some restoration was attempted by the Burgh Council in around 1954 and the grounds were laid out as an informal park with flower beds and seating areas.

---

3 Depending on the words of grant, further pleadings might be necessary to make clear that no public trust existed.

6. The Subjects have accordingly been used in part for the administration of the Burgh, although the requirement for the building to be used for that purpose has now passed following rationalisation. Following closure of Toff House itself in 2004, the building has been kept wind and watertight. The remainder of the Subjects have been dedicated to a public recreational use. However, that purpose has fallen into disuse with the residents of Deenburgh. Although a minimal degree of maintenance has been kept up on the land surrounding Toff House, there has been no positive recreational use for many years. Such use by locals as there has been tends to be antisocial activity by youths necessitating police intervention. There has been no request made to the Petitioners until very recently for any of the land, including the tennis court, to be restored to its former condition[4].

7. Following rationalisation of the Division formerly occupying the Subjects by the Petitioners, there is no longer a requirement for the Subjects to be maintained in local authority ownership. As condescended above, public recreational use of the land surrounding Toff House has ceased. As no other department of the Petitioners requires the building or the land for any other purpose, the Petitioners seek to dispose of the property for the best price that can reasonably be obtained. Given the residential character of the surrounding land, it is thought that this can be achieved by selling the land for housing. Consultations have been held with the Planning Authority which suggests that such a use would be acceptable to them.

8. Representations have been received by the Petitioners following the announcement of their plans to market the Subjects for housing from local residents who are aware of the provision in the title. One group, Toff House Action, have unveiled plans at a joint public meeting with the Gertrude Hyde Preservation Society for restoration of the grounds to the original design,

---

4 This is dangerous ground for the authority. Is it pleading its own neglect? In the face of opposition, the court might well require proof of how well maintained or otherwise the house and grounds had been.

with Toff House being used for community meeting rooms. The Petitioners have been in discussions with the group on the availability of funding for such a venture, and its long term financial viability[5].

9. The Petitioners believe that it is to the benefit of the residents of Deenburgh that the said land should be disposed of for the best price that can reasonably be obtained. Said disposal will generate a substantial capital receipt which will be used for the residents of Deenburgh. The Petitioners accordingly respectfully Petition the Court to authorise the disposal of the Subjects on such terms and conditions as the Court shall deem proper.

---

5 It has been assumed here that the proposal for restoration, whilst attracting local support, has still to reach some kind of maturity in terms of a business plan and funding. Toff House Action might consider moving the court to put off a decision until these matters have been finalised one way or another.

PLEAS-IN-LAW

1. Having regard to all the circumstances that the Petition be granted subject to such terms and conditions that the Court may deem fitting.

IN RESPECT WHEREOF

Solicitor
Deenburgh
Agent for the Petitioner.

PETITION

of

THE UTOPIA COUNCIL

for

Authority to alienate land at
Toff House, Deenburgh, Utopia

2006.

UTOPIA COUNCIL
Utopia House
North Street
DEENBURGH

Appendix III

Style advertisements

Style Advertisement for a Court of Session Petition

THE UTOPIA COUNCIL
TOFF HOUSE, DEENBURGH

Notice is hereby given that a Petition was presented in the Court of Session on 3 December 2006 by THE UTOPIA COUNCIL, a Local Authority constituted under the Local Government etc (Scotland) Act 1994 and having its main offices at Utopia House, North Street, Deenburgh for an Order under section 75(2) of the Local Government (Scotland) Act 1973. By interlocutor dated 19 December 2006 Lord Balnagowan appoints all parties having an interest to lodge Answers thereto within 21 days after intimation, service and advertisement.

Head of Legal Services
Utopia Council,
Utopia House,
North Street, Deenburgh
UU1 7XL

Date: 20 December 2006

Note: the Petition seeks the consent of the Court to dispose of Toff House, Deenburgh. The Petition is necessary as the land is held on the Common Good Account and the title deeds require the land to be used for the benefit of the community of Deenburgh. A plan is available of the property to be disposed of. If any person wishes to see the plan or be provided with more detail on this proposal they should contact William Hutton, Administrative Assistant, at Utopia House, North Street, Deenburgh. Alternatively copies of the plan will be available at Deenburgh Public Library, Book-worm Lane, Deenburgh and at Legal Services Section, Pettifoggers Alley, Deenburgh during office hours. If any person wishes to object to this proposal they may do so by lodging written Answers in the Court of Session, Edinburgh no later than 21 days from the date of publication of this advert i.e. by 10 January 2007.

Style Advertisement for a Sheriff Court Summary Application

THE UTOPIA COUNCIL PUBLIC NOTICE
SALE OF TOFF HOUSE, DEENBURGH

Notice is hereby given that the Utopia Council has raised a petition at Deenburgh Sheriff Court, under section 75(2) of the Local Government (Scotland) Act 1973 for authority to alienate Toff House, Deenburgh.

Anyone having an interest in the said Petition and who wishes to object should make themselves known to the Sheriff Clerk, Deenburgh Sheriff Court, Blackscauseway, Deenburgh DR1 3BQ where a copy of the Petition may be obtained (Court Ref No. DB66/06) within 21 days of publication of this notice.

H Scrivener,
Solicitor,
Utopia Council,
Pettifoggers Alley,
Deenburgh.

Disposal, appropriation and alienation

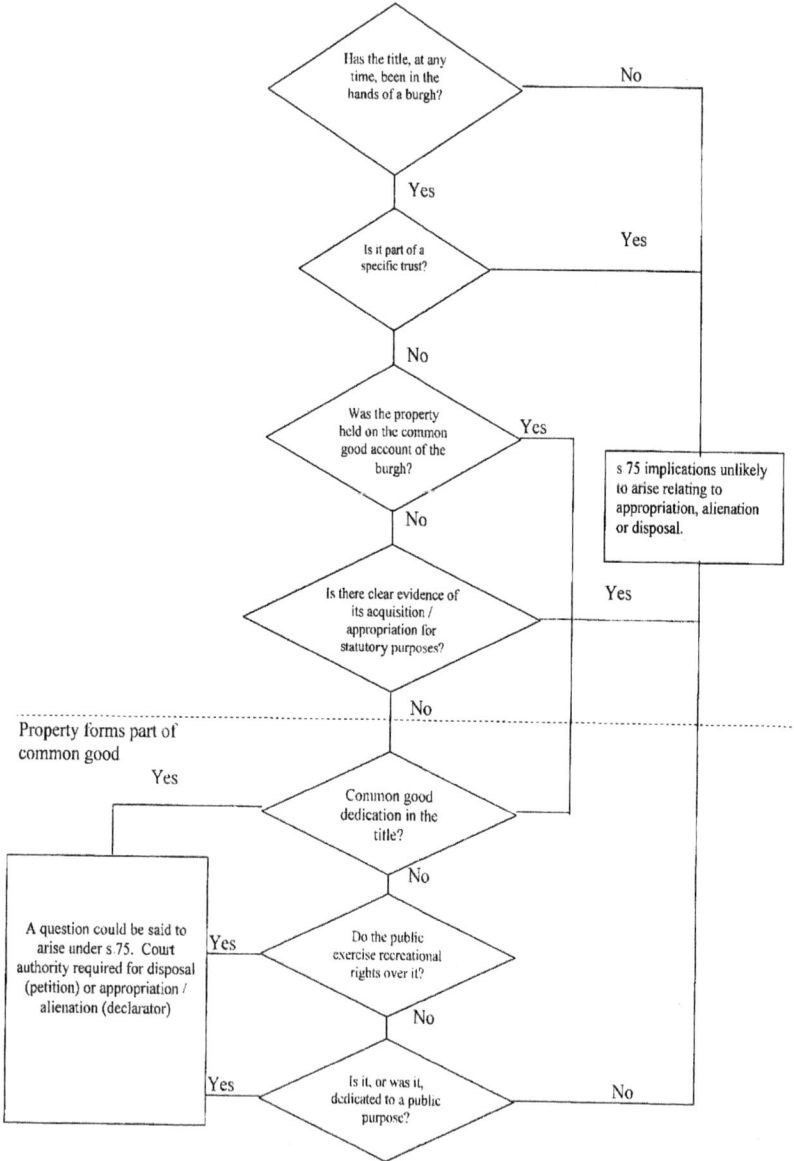

Has the title, at any time, been in the hands of a burgh? — No

Yes

Is it part of a specific trust? — Yes

No

Was the property held on the common good account of the burgh? — Yes

No

Is there clear evidence of its acquisition / appropriation for statutory purposes? — Yes

No

s 75 implications unlikely to arise relating to appropriation, alienation or disposal.

Property forms part of common good

Common good dedication in the title?

Yes

No

A question could be said to arise under s 75. Court authority required for disposal (petition) or appropriation / alienation (declarator)

Do the public exercise recreational rights over it? — Yes

No

Is it, or was it, dedicated to a public purpose? — Yes / No

Appendix V

Survey of local authorities on common good issues

In an attempt to gather data in relation to some common good issues, a survey was sent out in June 2005 via SOLAR contact lists to local authorities. Unfortunately, there were only nine responses so the results cannot claim to be statistically significant. If they show anything, it is that practices vary widely across the country.

1. **Administration of Common Good Funds**

(a) **Scheme of administration**
   How are matters relating to the common good taken at committee level?
   Full Council only
   Policy and Resources Committee/Other Strategic
      Committee   4
   Specific Common Good Sub-Committee   1
   Other[1]   3
   Finance and IT Resources Committee   1

(b) **How are decisions taken in relation to common good matters at official level? Is there a specific service responsibility?**
   Law and Administration   1
   Finance   2
   Other (please specify)[2]   6

---

1 Generally "other" has been a mixture of both full council and another committee, depending on the subject-matter.
2 Responses generally indicated either a corporate department/division, or a mixture of Law and Administration and Finance departments.

(c) **Assuming there is more than one former burgh in the local authority area, how is the common good fund administered?**

Separate fund for each former burgh	4
Amalgamated fund for all former burghs	2
No separate fund	1
Mixture of both	1
Not applicable	1

2. **Disposal of Common Good Property**

(a) **Since 1996, approximately how many separate burgh assets (land and/or buildings) have been disposed of?**

0–5	4
5–10	
10–20	1
Greater than 20	4

(b) **Of these, how many have thought to be part of the common good?**

0–5	6
5–10	
10–20	1
Greater than 20	2
All of them	

(c) **Of these, how many were thought to have required court consent?**

0–5	8
5–10	
10–20	
Greater than 20	
All of them	1

(d) **Of the cases which did require to go to court, how were expenses shared?**

Council bore all expenses	1
Expenses shared by objector/community council	1

A combination of the two   1[3]

(e) **Do you have any potential disposals of common good property? If so, please give details and specify if you consider a question may arise as to the Council's ability to dispose of the property.**

Of the four authorities responding to this question, one case concerned a former town hall, one a former plant nursery in a gifted park, one a country house, one a former school, and one an issue relating to charging for formal leisure facilities built on common good land.

3. <u>**Maintenance of Common Good Property**</u>

(a) **Where common good land or buildings require maintenance, who pays for it and from which budget?**

Occupying Service   1
Common Good   1
Other
Mixture   7

(b) **Do you consider your Council's treatment of maintenance issues in relation to common good property to be consistent?**

Yes   3
No   4
Not applicable[4]   1
No response   1

---

3 One other authority indicated that, wherever possible, expenses of the action were extracted from the purchaser of the property.
4 The "not applicable" related to an authority with virtually no common good land and buildings.

Index

Advancement of well-being, 29, 33, 34n, 98, 120

Advertisement
court actions, 124–25
style—
  Court of Session petition, 142–43
  sheriff court application, 143

Alienation
advancement of well-being, 98, 120
appropriation and, 95
common good, from, 83–84
common law, at, 19, 90, 94–95, 97
court approval, 119–20
demolition as, 91, 92–93
disposal distinguished, 88
interruption of use, 107
limitations on—
  gifted property, 65–66, 85
  dedication for public use, 61–64, 85, 104–05
  use from time immemorial, 56–61, 85, 105
meaning, 87, 88, 92
"question arises"—
  case law, 100–03
  court's discretion, 100–03, 104
  interpretation, 99–100, 102
  interruption of use, 107
  land with no public use, 105–06
  no question arising, 105–07
  original purpose disappeared, 106–07
  previous judicial consideration, 101, 103–04, 106
  use from time immemorial, 105
  when arising, 103–05
previous alienations, 57–58, 61
private/public partnerships and, 97

Alienation—*contd*
restrictions, 89, 94
title wording, 104
*See also **Appropriation; Disposal of land***

Appropriation
advancement of well-being, 98, 120
alienation and, 95
case law, 94–95
common good, into, 17, 24
common law, at, 94–95, 97
court approval, 119–20
meaning, 87–88
restrictions, 89, 94–95
statutory provisions, 24
statutory purpose, for, 83–84, 87–88
when permitted, 88–89
*See also **Alienation; Disposal of land***

Best value
conflicting interests, 45
meaning, 44
obligation to secure, 25, 29, 34, 44–45

Burghs
abolition, 4, 20, 23, 38
barony, of, 7
boundaries, 10–11
burgh status, grant of, 2
challenges to, 4–5
civic administration, 3–4
common good—
  property falling into, 67–78
  property falling outwith, 79–85
common good fund, 3
corruption, 3–4, 6
dissolution, 20
feu ferme status, 3

149